# SUPERFOOD KITCHEN

## COOKING WITH NATURE'S MOST AMAZING FOODS

# SUPERFOOD KITCHEN

COOKING WITH NATURE'S MOST AMAZING FOODS

JULIE MORRIS

STERLING EPICURE

New York

STERLING EPICURE
New York

An Imprint of Sterling Publishing
387 Park Avenue South
New York, NY 10016

First published in 2011 as *Superfood Cuisine*

Additional photo credits:
pp viii, 46, 72-73, 114, 137, and back cover/bottom © Brendan Brazier
pp x-xi © Jackie Morris
pp 13, 22, 24, 38, 42 photographed by Zach Adelman © Navitas Naturals

ISBN 978-1-4549-0352-9

Distributed in Canada by Sterling Publishing
c/o Canadian Manda Group, 165 Dufferin Street
Toronto, Ontario, Canada M6K 3H6
Distributed in the United Kingdom by GMC Distribution Services
Castle Place, 166 High Street, Lewes, East Sussex, England BN7 1XU
Distributed in Australia by Capricorn Link (Australia) Pty. Ltd.
P.O. Box 704, Windsor, NSW 2756, Australia

For information about custom editions, special sales, and
premium and corporate purchases, please contact Sterling Special Sales
at 800-805-5489 or specialsales@sterlingpublishing.com.

Manufactured in China

2 4 6 8 10 9 7 5 3 1

www.sterlingpublishing.com

# CONTENTS

# A NOTE TO MY READERS

I could begin by stating, eyebrow-raised, that this book is the result of copious amounts of hard, treacherous work. But, well, then I'd just be lying. I *love* working with food. To me, few activities are more rewarding than combining the detailed science of nutrition with nature's rainbow of flavors to create truly amazing edibles, and sharing these discoveries with you.

Having been involved in the natural food industry for close to a decade now, I've had the good fortune to work with some of the best companies in the biz, learning—from the inside out—what makes a *great* food. But it wasn't until I began working (as a chef and educator) with a superfood company called Navitas Naturals that I discovered the special set of ingredients that would transform my entire culinary outlook. In fact, it's my work with Navitas that served as much of the inspiration for this book.

I mention Navitas because the embarkment of any new culinary (and/or healthy) adventure inevitably involves overcoming a few hurdles. One such hurdle is sourcing new ingredients. Although my recipes deliberately rely upon fresh produce that is readily available in most places, some of the pantry superfoods are still relatively new to the Western world and thus sometimes hard to locate or of variable quality. To simplify things, I've included an Ingredient Resources Guide—a collection of the superfood companies I've come to know and trust for quality, price, and availability. You can refer to this guide at the back of the book (page 228).

Another hurdle can be using new, unfamiliar ingredients. How do they function? How do they taste? What do they go with? Are they a waste of money? I hear you. Luckily, my activities with superfood companies over the years have enabled me to alleviate this uncertainty as well. To be blunt: I've made the messes so you can make the masterpieces. This book is about sharing superfood successes.

Still, there is one hurdle that remains deceptively daunting—price. If you're new to using superfoods, I'll admit, there can be a bit of initial sticker shock. But keep in mind: These foods are so nutritionally concentrated, you'll only need to use a small amount to enjoy the benefits. In other words, they last! Camu powder, for example, may appear expensive, and yet just a pinch provides around 300 percent of the Recommended Daily Allowance (RDA) of vitamin C, which equates to less than 30 cents a serving per day. Unlike, say, a box of cereal, these foods are dense with the best nutrients nature has to offer, with the invaluable potential to energize and heal. Nothing feels as good as optimum health, and, cliché aside: yeah, you're worth it.

Many of these foods have been treasured since ancient times. Now, based on current nutrition research, we can appreciate these foods more than ever before. The overwhelming benefits of nature's most amazing foods are nothing short of revolutionary, and I'm honored to accompany you on your culinary exploration of them.

—*Julie Morris*

# BREAKING HABITS

Just a few weeks into college, I made a new best friend.

Coffee.

Of course, at the time, I had no idea our one-cup meeting at the small shop around the corner from my house would develop into such a close relationship.

I had just begun attending a design school in Southern California to study advertising. Far from your "free-love" style of art school, this institution was absolutely fierce with both competition and talent. The combination of nauseatingly brilliant peers and top-level professors, along with a new family of student loans that seemed to multiply like bacteria, quickly transformed me from a kid who simply liked to draw into a stress-infused, in-it-to-win-it workhorse.

The first thing I learned in art school is that creativity is a fickle beast. Sometimes it happily gushes out, and the world is covered in glitter, warm hugs, and dancing ponies. Other times, creativity decides to bail and go on vacation (inevitably around deadlines), and I'll tell you: the sound of those mental crickets can be deafening. I knew that to succeed in such a creatively demanding environment, I simply had no time for these "vacations"—I needed consistent energy to perform to the very best of my ability. Naturally, I found myself at coffee's doorstep.

There's a reason that coffee is the second most traded commodity on earth (oil is the first): coffee works. From its ability to keep me working away late into the night, to enabling a semi-conscious state of being the next day, coffee appeared to be a trustworthy friend. I'd have a cup or two throughout the day, and everything was dandy.

Then a problem surfaced. Since my heavy workload wasn't exactly slowing down anytime soon, my little cup of joe was now a habit I had to maintain. And to make matters worse, coffee had begun to lose its "kick." The cup that once gave me the energy I needed soon had to be doubled just to get the same effect. Then tripled. Not to mention I began experiencing wild energy swings—ups, downs, superhero-style, zombie-mode, annoying person who talks too fast, annoying person who never talks—all kinds of wacky states that inevitably drained my productivity as I attempted to keep everything "balanced." Finally, almost mockingly, coffee stopped working completely. I would drink a cup and ironically feel *more* tired. I had no idea what was going on. So of course, I did the next, most logical thing.

I didn't stop drinking coffee (don't be ridiculous), but instead tacked on an energy drink habit to my position as a full-time java junkie. As a twenty-year old, it really seemed like a great plan:

caffeine from the coffee, caffeine from the energy drink, all the other stimulant "mystery ingredients" from the energy drink, and a heck of a lot of sugar. Good times.

As you've likely already figured out, this little exercise of mine didn't exactly go over so well either. Sure, initially—for a couple of weeks—things were "amazing." I was back on my feet and buzzing around like someone had hit the fast-forward button. But, as if experiencing energy karma, I soon crashed . . . and this time, crashed really hard. My energy hit rock bottom right at the end of a semester, and as a result, I could barely function well enough to get my final projects finished, let alone be as successful as I had anticipated. Feeling like a person much older than my actual age, I ended the school year exhausted, experiencing chronic stomach pains, overall achiness, and, most frustrating of all, I found my productivity was completely shot. I needed a change.

Luckily, nutrition was something that had always interested me. Well, no. Let me rephrase that. *Food* was something that had always interested me; nutrition came later. To my young self's credit, years of culinary enjoyment and research had already morphed my cheese-gorging episodes into embracing a beneficial plant-based lifestyle—which I was quite proud of for environmental, health, and ethical reasons. But even this improvement still included a lot of highly processed foods that just happened not to include the ingredients I was looking to avoid. As luck would have it, right around the time of my personal "energy crisis," I had started reading about these strange things called "superfoods." The image of a grape with a cape began to creep into my psyche.

Superfoods really did seem to be awfully attractive. Here they were—foods that had been used for thousands and thousands of years, among cultures all around the world, fist-pumped and high-fived millions of times (I'm sure) for their profoundly rejuvenating properties. Plus, they provided natural energy. Sold.

After nerdily large amounts of research, I finally settled in on two superfoods with which to begin my new energy-driven experiment: maca and goji berries. They were both strange-sounding foods—one was a powder made from a dehydrated brown root popular in South American culture; the other was a bag of dried red berries utilized in Chinese medicine. Not exactly anything to salivate over, but worth a shot nonetheless. Admittedly, I had no idea what to do with them. A friend suggested I try making simple "energy balls"—little rolled globes of maca, goji berries, some kind of nut butter, and a sweetener, all mixed together. They were decent tasting, I suppose . . . a little on the ugly side . . . but as I chowed down on my new snack, I imagined some ancient Mayan medicine man giving me a thumbs-up and was inspired.

To allow the superfoods to work to their full potential, I decided I needed to give coffee and all other stimulant drinks the boot. So with energy balls in hand, I gave myself a month to experience "the wonders of superfoods."

The first thing I noticed was, well, nothing. I didn't get that heightened buzz or extreme rush of energy that I had become accustomed to from coffee. Frankly, this disappointed me. But also included in this "nothing" was not feeling tired, or having to deal with a mental slump. In fact, after just a couple of weeks, I felt just generally *good*—not any extreme ups, but not any extreme downs, either. Just consistent, even energy that served as the perfect base for me to focus on the things I actually wanted to focus on. It was then that I fully understood that food could have two very important roles: taste and function.

Oh, without question I understand the seduction of taste-only foods: the wild banshee call of a rich, chocolate brownie . . . or the frenzied pursuit of a salty/crunchy/munchie fix needed for *immediate* consumption. Been there, and rest assured, I'm not going to get out the soapbox and whine about how bad junk foods are, because yeah, we know that already. Yet there's one other unexpected benefit (outside of just extra energy) of incorporating more of these nutrient-dense natural foods into a diet: diminished cravings.

Personally, it wasn't that my cravings went away (my "brownienthusiasm" is still as strong as ever); I just crave different things now. For example, after only a couple of months of eating whole, nutrient-rich foods, chowing down on a "conventional" brownie began to make me feel like I was ingesting sludge (likely due to its high content of cane sugar, unhealthy fats, and refined flours with no nutritional value). This was a food that was doing nothing to benefit me, and though it might score a ten on taste, it was a zero on function. But rather than banish brownies and sweets for life (that's no fun), I simply found new ways to make some of my favorite goodies using foods that were night-and-day better for well-being. My recipes began to take on a whole new shape as I focused first on the function of each ingredient—what it could do for me; how it could support my health; how it could energize and balance my body—and then went to town on making it taste amazing. The effortless weight maintenance, clear skin, and increased athleticism that followed told me I was doing something right.

So, while my crazy days in advertising have come and gone, I'm still no stranger to coveting simple recipes that can fuel an energetic lifestyle. Initially created out of my own need for casual, crave-worthy cuisine I could be proud to enjoy, the recipes included in these pages give tribute to superfoods of all shapes and sizes—the yes-please pick-me-ups of the foodie world. Whether you're a natural food connoisseur or just waiting for the pizza dude to deliver, this new repertoire of simple recipes is composed of life-enhancing, energy-giving, delicious natural food choices that will make your taste buds *and* your body smile. The new generation of cooking is looking bright, and it begins with superfoods.

# PART ONE

# UNDERSTANDING SUPERFOODS

# THE EXPERIENCE OF EATING

The year is 2,000,000 BC. Well, somewhere around there. Let's just call it pre-Homo erectus time. Over there, by that tree, is Mr. HominoidAncestralPerson. Next to him, his lovely partner Mrs. HominoidAncestral-Person; and that short and cute hairy fellow is their five year old son, HominoidAncestral-Person Jr. Much like the other primates in the area, these family members generally stick to themselves. Mr. and Mrs. H. see "the others" in the area, but, for the most part, they spend their time gathering plant-based grub and occasionally catching an animal for food. The rest of their time is spent being over-zealous parents, keeping everything and everyone away from their precious offspring, much like the protective apes and chimpanzees in the area. There's not much need for any further interaction with others.

Then, *kazaam*. Along comes the discovery of fire, and with it, a three-fold benefit. First, it provides warmth and light. Second, it keeps larger predators away at night. And lastly—cue the trumpets—it enables the cooking of food. Suddenly, it's time to gather around, all you hominoid families. You have an activity in common: cooking.

Some sociologists believe that absolutely paramount to our social evolution was the event of cooking, because for the very first time in history, early humans had a reason to consistently collect together and connect with one another. Thus, hanging out around the ancient "fireplace" was in fact where we developed our first social skills—an ideal way to pass the time with everyone sitting around together waiting for food to cook. Sounds like a pretty nice way to spend an evening, no? I think so, too. True to our roots, today's world continues to maintain a close connection between the preparation of food and social activities, both formal and casual.

Sure, the preparation of food has evolved a bit from our primal days (college students excepted). That caveman probably wasn't too concerned about his chocolate ganache being overly sweet or getting his pasta just al dente. Nowadays, whether it's dinner from a takeout container or a garden pea soup made from scratch, food preparation involves a lot more thought than simply relying on a freshly stoked fire to work its magic. Most chefs believe that in understanding how to make food, we must first understand the *experience* of food. And this experience revolves around three oh-so-important sensory points that are the hallmark of a "properly" created dish: sight, smell, and taste.

Sensory point one, sight, makes sense; the better a food looks, the more tempting it becomes.

We look for attractive colors, familiar shapes, and some form of organization that suggests the cook made a dish especially for us, because we're clearly quite lovely.

Sensory point two comes with a party trick: bite into an apple, a potato, and then an onion with your nose plugged. They taste almost identical. Life would be pretty bland without the sense of smell. And regardless of whether you're smelling food consciously (as when wine tasting) or unconsciously (such as taking a breath before eating a bite), enticing smells can promote a favorable food experience. Astute chefs will often use fragrant herbs and essences that play more of a role in scent than they do in flavor, convincing our nose to send signals up to the brain that let us know "this is gonna be good."

You're probably way ahead of me now on sensory point number three: taste. Obviously, the final judgment rests with the taste buds in our mouth, which efficiently categorize our food with a "love-it" or "hate-it" verdict almost instantaneously. Both flavor and "mouth feel" (texture) go hand in hand to have the last word on what we eat.

And as far as classic modern cuisine goes, that's the road map to a great dish. Kitchen closed.

Or is it?

A superfood staple: leafy green vegetables.

Notice that there's a problem with this philosophy of eating: it's profoundly shortsighted. The food experience doesn't simply stop after a good chew. That's like walking up to a baseball plate, assessing the pitch, experiencing the crack of your bat hitting the ball . . . and then assuming the game is over. Obviously, the all-important field reaction to the hit still needs to happen, and that's when the real game begins.

One of my very first jobs in college was working at lunchtime in a nice Italian restaurant. At the end of each shift, I would always look forward to ordering an item off the menu—usually a wood-fired cheese pizza or some kind of crazy good pasta. The food always tasted stellar, and the fact that it was a complimentary perk of working at the restaurant was certainly a benefit to my (lack of) budget. But I had one ongoing problem: every day after my lunch, right around 3:00, I would feel sleepy, lethargic, and unable to concentrate. I found this especially annoying as the fatigue hit right after I left work and went to finish my homework for class. "Oh, well, you just ate," was the common answer when I explained my problem to people. The ultimate reaction to a good meal—feeling tired, unproductive, or even experiencing physical discomfort—was accepted as perfectly normal. Really?

It could be argued that in some ways our ancestors instinctively understood food better than we do today, as they sought out foods that provided long-lasting energy and sustenance as opposed to focusing solely on flavor and pleasure.

Regardless, one thing is clear: most contemporary food preparation leaves out a fundamental aspect of the experience of eating—how food makes us feel.

## EATING FOR ENERGY

Without getting into the nitty-gritty intricacies of nutrition, it's important to understand food on its most basic level. Why do we eat? Outside of cravings, temptations, social customs, boredom, etc., why do we actually consume food?

It all comes down to energy. The pang of hunger we feel is simply the body's request for fuel, so that it can produce energy. We're instinctively attracted to calorie-dense foods to most efficiently propel our activities—including mental activities! (The brain taps 25 percent of the body's energy.) Even the very definition of a calorie is nothing more than a unit of energy. So the fact that our modern food choices often make us sleepy, mentally unfocused, fat, or even sick, is a huge red flag: there's something seriously wrong with what we're eating.

On the flip side, *good* food rejuvenates us. Good food supports our activities, keeps us healthy, keeps us strong, and keeps us at our prime. I'm pretty sure the scientific explanation for eating good food is simply, "you: now with more awesome." And it's with this mind-set—preparing food with sight, smell, taste, and *energy* all taken simultaneously into consideration—that you have the makings of a Superfood Kitchen.

# WHAT IS A SUPERFOOD?

Few people can resist a seductive mango. Smooth juicy flesh. Enticing tropical aroma. Attention-grabbing orange hue. And a magnificently complex flavor, ranging from floral to honey to the encapsulated flavor of "vacation." Ahhh. The mango is a recipe via nature—and a brilliant one at that. But on top of its sweet taste and fun texture, the mango has another gift in store: it's phenomenally rich in nutrients. Mangos contain a bountiful supply of vitamin C, vitamin A, potassium, and beta carotene. They're also an excellent source of an antioxidant known as lupeol, which is found inside the mango pulp. Lupeol has been shown in preliminary studies to suppress tumor growth as well as reduce kidney stones—which is pretty amazing stuff. So all of that delicious goodness aside, the potent nutritional power of the friendly mango catapults it from good fruit to bona fide superfood.

Admittedly, "superfood" is a term that has been increasingly tossed around in the marketplace. The word was officially coined back in 1915, when it made its first appearance in the Oxford English Dictionary as simply "a food considered especially nutritious or otherwise beneficial to health and well-being." Nowadays, the official definition has been tweaked ever so slightly to read, "a nutrient-rich food considered to be especially beneficial for health and well-being."

With such a catchy name—*super* (yay!) plus *food* (yum!)—and currently no official boundaries on verbiage claims, it's easy to see how such a term would become exploited as a flashy selling point, with food companies and marketing professionals attempting to make their products seem more beneficial (i.e., sugary cereal . . . now with *superfoods!*). In Europe, the problem of this misleading hype became so prevalent, the European Union banned using the term "superfood" on products that do not clearly provide some kind of credible scientific documentation to back up the claim. With no legal standards currently established on the definition of superfoods, this kind of negative press undoubtedly puts superfoods more in the collective ranks of Bigfoot and other myths, as opposed to a celebrated natural discovery and useful health tool.

Semantics and over-zealous advertisers aside, the concept behind superfoods remains very real. I personally define a superfood as a natural food containing an exceptionally high nutrient density, as well as phytochemicals and antioxidants. Yet to really understand superfoods beyond just the yay/yum factor, we have to look at them a little more closely and find out what exactly sets them apart from the rest of the food kingdom.

## HISTORICAL USE

Likely, you've seen it: the news headlines in a PR flurry with some "discovery" of a new natural superfood with the exciting ability to balance, energize, and heal our bodies. But the truth is, most superfoods were "discovered" long ago. Really long ago. In fact, many ancient cultures from all around the world are now credited with first recognizing the powerful potential in some fruits, roots, seeds, plants, and berries. So yes, it seems *everyone* was eating superfoods back then.

It was around 10,000 years ago that humans first got the whole "farming" thing down—most likely beginning with figs, and then moving on to grains. With the progress of agriculture, many superfoods were selected as the go-to crops. Archaeological records show that flaxseed was sown in ancient Babylon for over 5,000 years, and chia seeds were a well-known staple food of Aztec warriors. Acai berries were used in early Amazonian folk medicine, and in more recent history hemp was one of the first vital crops grown in the American colonies before the revolution, with farmers even required by law to grow the mighty plant.

I believe that the reason superfoods were so prevalent in the past is largely due to the fact that food was harder to grow and not as readily available, so it only made sense for our ancestors to cultivate crops and forage foods that offered the most "bang for their buck." And though these cultures may not have had the means to perform fancy scientific testing and medical reviews (measuring the quantity of specific nutrients in a food, etc.), that wasn't important for their purposes. Instead, these "less sophisticated" cultures were able to empirically discern which foods made them feel good, have

more energy, and perform better—all by simply listening to their bodies.

Meanwhile, as modern culture has evolved, our food, ironically, has not. It goes without saying that we have an exciting amount to learn from the simpler, more natural diets of civilizations long before us.

## FUNCTIONAL FOOD

Here's a mini-mantra: ask not what you can do to your food, but what your food can do for you! Indeed, a functional food is essentially just what it sounds like: a food that supports a well-functioning organism. And guess what? Every superfood fits into this category. These foods have extra nutritional perks that do more than just taste good—they have a valuable effect on the body as well. If we eat a handful of goji berries, for example, we're getting loads of antioxidants, vitamins, minerals, a little protein, and healthy carbohydrates, all in the package of a sweet treat. These well-balanced goji berries have essential phytonutrients (plant-based nutrients) that our bodies can use to support functions like eyesight and the immune system. A plate of traditional fettuccine, on the other, offers us little more than, well . . . carbohydrates. (Thanks?) The nutritional superiority of superfoods is easy to see: these functional foods are more than just calories; they're foods with real-deal benefits.

## PREVENTATIVE MEDICINE

A few years back, sixty men and women—half of whom were smokers—participated in a clinical study involving antioxidants in food. Each day, they were required to eat one small bowl full of leafy green watercress in addition to their normal diet. The impressive results, as published in the American Journal of Clinical Nutrition, showed that both groups (smokers and non-smokers) enjoyed increased ability to resist the damage of free radicals. This is great news, for as you may know, free radicals are destructive, highly unstable molecules that can cause damage and cell death to occur. Associated with aging and degenerative diseases, an excess of free radicals in the body is often the result of a high exposure to pollution, radiation, chemicals, or toxins like cigarette smoke. Professor Ian Rowland, who led the study, explains the connection, "blood cell DNA damage is an indicator of whole body cancer risk, and the results support the theory that consumption of [cruciferous vegetables like] watercress is linked to an overall reduced risk of cancer at various sites in the body." These findings are the very essence of preventative medicine: enlisting the help of a healthy habit (in this case, eating nutrient-dense watercress) to increase protection against preventable disease.

Interestingly, the researchers also discovered that the highest level of beneficial change recorded was, in fact, among the smoker group. The phytochemicals in the watercress provided so much antioxidant protection that they brought each person's individual chemistry into balance— providing greater relief to those with higher levels of free radicals caused by their unhealthy habits. This concept is empowering in its implication that it's never too late to benefit from incorporating elements of healthy eating into our lifestyle.

It's easy to see how, once we get past the narrow confines of Western medicine, the lines between food, herbs, and medicine often overlap. That's not to say that heredity and environmental factors play no role in long-term health, but feeding our bodies top-quality ingredients keeps us in prime condition and maximizes our ability to battle any ailment—from a sprained ankle to a degenerative disease. Many people notice that after maintaining a superfood-infused lifestyle, they get sick less frequently, and recover more quickly when something nasty does strike. In short, a diet full of superfoods lets us enjoy the healthy lifestyle we crave.

## NUTRIENT DENSITY

### NUTRIENT DENSITY RATIO
### NUTRIENTS : CALORIES

On the surface, nutrition appears to be quite the complex beast (and probably a little boring). I've read arguments for, and against, almost every food in the world. Not surprisingly, more and more people say, "I *want* to be healthy, but I don't know how." Maybe you've heard it. Maybe you've said it. Luckily, understanding the basics of nutrition (i.e. what to eat) is amazingly simple. It really comes down to one core concept: nutrient density. Understand this idea, and it becomes crystal clear why superfoods really stand out and shine.

Simply put, nutrient density is the ratio of micronutrients to calories. A food with high calories and relatively low nutrients, like a piece of cheese, will have a low nutrient density ratio. On the flip side, a food with low calories and a high amount of nutrients, like blueberries, will have a high nutrient density score. High nutrient density = good. Low nutrient density = bad. Easy enough.

Of course, it's important to understand what "nutrients" are. Ask any guy on the street, and he'll likely describe "nutrition" as a class of nutrients known as macronutrients: protein, fat, and carbohydrates. While essential to our well being, macronutrients only provide the calories that our body uses as fuel. They're ubiquitous in food: every edible thing on the planet (with the exception of water and chemicals) has one, two, or all three of these macronutrients, so it isn't any big party when a food contains them.

What's important in the case of nutrient density, however, is a separate class of nutrition known as micronutrients. These involve exactly what their name implies: nutrients we need in only very small quantities. While we don't need them in massive amounts (like the heavy-duty calorie sources we run on), don't be fooled—they're absolutely essential. The World Health Organization (WHO) explains, "even though they are only needed in miniscule amounts, these substances are the 'magic wands' that enable the body to produce enzymes, hormones, and other substances that are essential for proper growth and development." WHO also warns, "As tiny as these amounts are, the consequences of their absence are severe." To be more blunt, a diet without micronutrients equals disease, premature aging, loss of bodily functions, and all-around degeneration. Micronutrients are our tiny heroes in the nutrition spectrum.

There's a vast array of nutritional components that live under the umbrella of the micronutrient family. The most commonly known are vitamins, macrominerals (essential minerals we need a lot of), and trace minerals (essential minerals we need a little of). But equally important in this family are organic acids, antioxidants, and a broad range of other organic compounds known as phytochemicals—plant chemicals—which, though not essential, appear to offer numerous health benefits. Because there are so many micronutrients (scientists estimate there may be as many as 100,000 different kinds of phytochemicals, with over a hundred often contained in a single plant), it's virtually impossible to even try and compare one nutrient-dense food to another as generally "better" or "worse." The nutrients in every natural food each have a different, yet important role that contributes to overall balance (health). What focusing on micronutrients does allow us to determine, however, is whether eating a certain food is a smart choice for our diet. Confused about nutrition? Look for micronutrient quantity. By seeking these little superheroes, it becomes easy to weed out poor choices, and instead include other foods that gleam with benefits (such as almost *all* whole foods in the plant-based kingdom)! And most inspiring are a specific group of these beneficial foods that clearly rise to the very top of the edible ranks, practically overflowing with nutritional power. Indeed, this top stratum defines superfoods.

## THE ANDI SYSTEM

Of course, using the concept of nutritional density requires knowing what nutrients a specific food contains in the first place. And for those who'd (understandably) rather leave the research to someone else, utilizing the ANDI nutrition rating system removes much of the guesswork. Developed by Dr. Joel Fuhrman, a natural physician, best-selling author, and founder of Eat Right America, the ANDI system (which stands for Aggregate Nutrient Density Index) works to rank foods based on their nutrient density ratio on a scale of 1 (worst) to

1000 (best). The system evaluates an extensive range of micronutrients, including (but not limited to) vitamins, minerals, phytochemicals, and antioxidants. While an ideal diet comes through eating an assortment of nutrient-rich foods, the ANDI system is currently among the most comprehensive methods of uncovering the best ingredients for optimal health. Though not all specialty superfoods have yet been included, based on their nutrition in comparison to ANDI-rated foods, it's easy to gauge how highly they would rank. Also, at this time, only whole food ingredients are measured using this system—no snacks, recipes, processed, or packaged foods are listed.

Of course, the ANDI rating system is not a black-and-white answer to nutrition. Important to note is that some foods rate lower in the system due to being more caloric (such as higher fat foods, like nuts) yet still offer tremendous benefits. This is because the ANDI system does not recognize the *source* of calories while determining a food's score (such as good fats versus bad fats, refined sugars versus natural ones, etc.)—only the *number* of calories. If a person were to eat nothing but the foods residing in the top tier of the ANDI charts, the resulting diet would unquestionably be far too low in calories, lack a healthy amount of fat, and contain many other imbalances as well. So, while I recommend utilizing the findings of the ANDI system as a wonderful guide for confirming some premium food choices (like leafy greens and berries, for example), I encourage even more the appreciation and application of its overall *concept*: eating a variety of whole foods, with a focus on acquiring as many micronutrients as possible.

While the ANDI system is not the only indication of a phenomenal food, it certainly goes a long way to pointing us in the right direction.

## SAMPLE ANDI SCORES

| | |
|---|---|
| Collard Greens | 1000 |
| Kale | 1000 |
| Watercress | 1000 |
| Bok Choy | 824 |
| Spinach | 739 |
| Arugula | 559 |
| Broccoli | 376 |
| Strawberries | 212 |
| Pomegranate Juice | 193 |
| Lentils | 104 |
| Flaxseeds | 65 |
| Tofu | 37 |
| Ground beef | 20 |
| White bread | 18 |
| Cheddar cheese | 11 |
| Cola | 1 |

From EatRightAmerica.com—see this website for the ANDI list in full.

## NUTRITION IN THE KITCHEN

A person should not need a degree in nutrition just to understand how to eat well, and these fundamental nutrition concepts make the "good food road map" simple and accessible. Needless to say, when creating the recipes for *Superfood Kitchen,* I set out to marry the best of two worlds: the enticing fusion of the flavors and textures of "cuisine," with the philosophies of a nutrient-rich diet. The resulting recipes not only contain a boost from exciting "superfoods," but also make overall healthy ingredient choices, so the recipe as a whole offers broad-spectrum nutrition. I suppose, in a way, each dish could be considered a superfood in and of itself . . . representing the sum of a collection of some very super parts.

# THE NEED FOR NUTRIENT DENSITY

No one will disagree that eating more whole foods is a smart move to promote a heathier body. Yet one question I continually hear is whether such an intense focus on nutrient density is really essential. Isn't simply eating more natural foods—such as potatoes, rice, or corn—enough? While these foods are certainly leaps and bounds ahead of processed fare, the proof of big-picture health is undeniably in the superfood pudding: when we eat nature's first-rate foods, we enable our body to function in first-rate fashion—promoting optimum health, energy, mental clarity, and resistance to disease. And today, more than ever before, we have increasingly urgent reasons to pursue the abundant rewards of superfoods. Here's why.

## THE RELATIONSHIP OF DIET AND DISEASE

Modern medicine has certainly made tremendous strides in fighting disease. Yet for the very first time in history, a younger generation is showing signs of a shorter life expectancy than its parent generation. Epidemic rates of terminal diseases such as heart disease, diabetes, cancer, osteoporosis, obesity—to name just a few—are at an all-time high, and rising.

The problem stems largely from our current Western diet: a profound dependence on processed and refined (nutrient-void) foods, which inundate our bodies with empty calories; a habitual craving for animal protein, with its cholesterol-forming saturated fats and destructive acidic impact on our blood chemistry; and the almost unconscious consumption of refined sugars (such as high fructose corn syrup and excessive white cane sugar), whose omnipresence on supermarket shelves has contributed to the alarming spike in diabetes, among many other diseases. Our addiction to these foods is literally destroying us. Because they often require more resources from the body just to digest than they give back in benefits, these foods can be classified as "antinutrients." Instead of building us up, they actually break us down: robbing our body of energy (just think how you feel after a "heavy meal"), as well as leaching our existing stores of nutrients from various organs, bones, etc. during the digestive process. Hence, the consumption of antinutrient foods leaves us in the red with an ugly nutrient deficit . . . essentially putting out a welcome mat for disease.

But the forecast doesn't have to be so grim. There's power in prevention, and the potential for the body to renew itself is miraculous when supplied with the tools it needs. Modern studies point to the utilization of a whole-food, plant-based diet as one of the most promising ways to keep these serious—yet largely preventable—chronic diseases at bay. For example, the World Cancer Research Fund has stated that simply by eating the right diet, a person can cut his or her cancer risk by up to 40 percent (a number thought to be on the conservative side by many estimates).

Here to help—in a dramatic way—are super-foods: one of the easiest, most efficient ways to make significant beneficial changes to even the most risky of lifestyles. Small, powerful changes really do add up, and superfoods are one of the best ways to make an impact.

## PH BALANCE

You don't have to be a chemist to understand the concept behind eating for a balanced pH . . . which is a good thing, as pH is vital to the generation of life. Likely, you're already somewhat familiar with the pH scale: the acid/alkaline balance using the pH scale of 1–14. (Sneak review: a pH of 0–7 is considered acidic, while anything above 7 is considered alkaline—also sometimes referred to as basic.) When speaking of health and wellness, most important is to remember the slightly alkaline range of 7.35–7.45, the pH levels at which the human body is considered "balanced."

Maintaining a perfect pH is not as biologically rhythmic as, say, breathing. Instead, the body must constantly adapt to maintain its equilibrium, as it is affected by every single food and beverage that is consumed (even water!). Once metabolized, food is broken down into an ash residue that registers as acid or alkaline, and directly influences our biological pH "soup." Most Western diets do no favors

to balancing pH levels, since they're overflowing in acid-forming foods like meat, dairy, sugar, grains, coffee, etc. Including too many acidic foods puts a tremendous strain on the body as it struggles to balance its pH levels, which can result in weakened bones, declines in kidney function, premature aging, increased susceptibility to diseases, and more. (An overly alkaline environment is not desirable either, but very rare.)

Among the most alkaline foods are vegetables (especially anything green), and some fruits. Many superfoods fall within this category and even the ones that don't (seeds, for example) still refrain from dipping too deeply below the acid mark. The key word really is *balance*, and superfoods can help keep us in the sweet spot, relieving our body of its pH "fight" and letting it focus on other things like providing energy and healing. While there's no need to become obsessed with constantly maintaining the "perfect pH," seeking as much alkaline-forming food as possible is a huge step in our quest for health and longevity.

## DEFENSE AGAINST ENVIRONMENTAL TOXINS

The approximate number of man-made chemicals released into the environment annually: 50,000. The number of gallons of pesticides and herbicides applied each year to our food supply: 500,000,000. The number of new man-made chemicals (which encompasses pesticides, antibiotics, and hormone residues) added into manufactured food since just 1950: 3,500.

Choosing organic whole foods is one of the very best decisions a consumer can make to protect against chemicals, to avoid genetically modified

A Peruvian outdoor market offering local superfoods like quinoa, maca, and sacha inchi.

foods, and to send a monetary message to the companies who use chemicals at the expense of public health. By exercising the power of your dollar, you can tell these profiteers that their products will not be tolerated and will not be purchased.

Unfortunately, even supporting organic food is not 100 percent foolproof. Over time, chemicals accumulate in the environment and drift from their initial point of application. These chemicals permeate our environment and, eventually, our food—sometimes with toxic repercussions.

The best defense against the rising tide of pesticides is to consume antioxidants, which are found in almost all plant-based foods in varying levels. Measured in ORAC units (which stands for Oxygen Radical Absorbance Capacity), the term "antioxidant" does not actually indicate a class of nutrients itself, like the mineral or vitamin families, but instead describes a functional capacity some nutrients demonstrate for fighting free radicals. Nutrients that contain antioxidant properties can range from the anti-inflammatory class of phenolic acids (like the ellagic acid found in pomegranates), to important minerals like selenium, to the all-essential vitamin C. Some antioxidants, like the flavonoid and carotenoid families, are even responsible for the way many foods look and taste. Bright natural colors—from the intense purple of maqui berries to the vibrant orange of a carrot to even the deep black hues of wild rice and black quinoa—are all an indication of antioxidant activity (all the more reason to eat the rainbow!). By helping to stave off oxidation and decay, antioxidants are absolutely essential to combat the toxic reality of today's industrialized world and to prevent disease.

Currently, the USDA has set our Recommended Daily Allowance (RDA) at 5,000 ORAC units. (Many nutritionists agree that this number is far lower than what we actually need; nonetheless most North Americans don't even come close to meeting the USDA's recommendation. Additionally, a person's size, activity level, health, and environment will all have an effect on this number.) By far, the most condensed natural source of antioxidants are superfoods. Just look at acai, for example: a two tablespoon serving of freeze-dried pure acai powder provides almost 4,700 ORAC units—just 300 units short of the entire RDA benchmark. Talk about making life easy! Rich in anti-inflammatories, potent with free-radical scavenging antioxidants, and packed with effective detoxifying phytochemicals (beneficial plant chemicals), superfoods act as a natural buffer to the dangers of poison and pollution.

## LESS BANG FOR THE BUCK: NUTRIENT LOSS IN PLANTS

A growing population demands a growing food supply, and North American industrial agriculture has succeeded in producing a soaring quantity of food. But the increased bulk has come at a cost: plants have dramatically lost nutrient density.

Reports now indicate that vegetables contain anywhere from 5 to 40 *fewer* nutrients than they did just fifty years ago.

This drastic decline is primarily due to large-scale monoculture agricultural systems, which, by planting the same crop over and over again, have created imbalances in the topsoil. Plants can only acquire nutrients that exist in the soil in which they grow. And with the cultivation of plants that boast a faster growing cycle, there isn't as much time to absorb the already diminished nutrients in the soil. Thus, our compromised produce is no mystery: degraded soils plus quick harvests produce a low-quality food. And low-quality food means having to consume more of it (more calories) to get the desired amount of nutrients.

Agriculture's history of genetic breeding to increase the size of produce (which yields a more profitable crop) has also contributed to a lower nutrition density. These bloated fruits and vegetables may look larger and more attractive than the ones our grandparents ate, but this larger size does not equate to a proportionate benefit in nutrition. Today's larger produce simply contains more "dry matter"—a term that primarily refers to simple carbohydrates—and not more nutrients. Once again, eating more calories (even from these "good foods") is required to get the same result.

These efforts to increase food production have resulted in natural food that is less nourishing. Luckily, most superfoods have not been subjected to this methodology, as they have never been popularized by Big Agriculture. And even the ones that have—like greens—still contain tremendous nutritional benefits. Superfoods are the answer to finding a natural low-calorie source of the nutrition that is desperately lacking in even the best of diets.

# PART TWO

# CREATING A SUPERFOOD KITCHEN

# THE NEW SUPERFOOD PANTRY

Throughout the book, this symbol ✳ represents a superfood.

Let's be honest: there's no such thing as the "Perfect Food." Natural foods—of superfood status or not—function as team players, each contributing a unique and complementary set of nutritional attributes (a key to why pursuing health through isolated synthetic vitamins is not particularly effective). Understandably, the mantra behind superfood cuisine is to promote a top quality *variety* of exciting edibles that together offer prime nutritional synergy.

Of course, looking at the core definition of a superfood alone, it's easy to see that a great number of vegetables, fruits, seeds, and other plant-based foods function in ways that would qualify them as worthy of wearing the "nutrient-dense" cape. Nonetheless, some superfoods are so profoundly packed with beneficial qualities, they deserve a closer look. It's not that they offer different nutrition than everyday plant-based whole foods per se; they just offer it in a dramatically higher concentration. Some of these foods are so nutrient-dense, they require as little as a spoonful to catapult an entire recipe into superfood status.

The following selection of cherry-picked "specialty superfoods" are chosen for their efficient contribution to living a healthy lifestyle. Though I'm finding these ingredients available in more and more local retail outlets due to an increase in superfood popularity, depending on where you live, you may need to do a little hunting to find some of them. Most, however, can be found in your neighborhood health food store, and if they don't carry an ingredient, put in a request to the manager to bring in this new item, or place a special order (you'll help make these foods a staple grocery item for everyone). Ordering non-perishable specialty ingredients online is also a fantastically easy option, and I've mapped out quality sources for each of the superfoods in this specialty section in the Ingredient Resources Guide (page 228). They are the sources that were used for the development of the recipes in this book.

Of course, this pantry is by no means a complete tally of all superfoods on the planet. The earth abounds with astoundingly healthy edibles, some of which are just being discovered. But for our kitchen purposes, the foods listed here have the golden combination of being more readily available, as well as more useful from a culinary (aka deliciousness potential) standpoint. This special pantry list is comprised of an extraordinary collection of culinary superstars.

# SPECIALTY SUPERFOODS

## ✳ ACAI BERRY

Dark purple and the size of a blueberry, acai berries grow in clusters on tall palm trees native to the Amazon rainforest. Ancient Amazonian tribes began using acai thousands of years ago, both medicinally and as food; more recently, it has become famous as an energy food among Brazilian surf cultures, fueling surfers' long active days on the beach. This small Amazonian berry ranks as one of nature's most concentrated sources of antioxidants, with twice the antioxidants of blueberries.

In addition to its exceptionally high ORAC value, acai's nutrition is enhanced by healthy monounsaturated and polyunsaturated fats (the same fats that make olive oil a healthy oil). Acai also contains a broad range of vitamins and minerals, plant sterols (which have been linked to lowering cholesterol), amino acids, and a naturally low sugar content.

*Flavor notes:* A unique unsweetened, mild blackberry flavor, with hints of chocolate and a delicate richness throughout.

*Recommended forms:* Freeze-dried acai powder, pure acai juice (avoid pre-sweetened brands, which contain an excess of added sweeteners), or unsweetened frozen acai pulp packs (sold in the freezer sections of some health food stores). Or, if you're in South America, rejoice and enjoy it fresh!

*Use in:* Breakfasts, drinks and smoothies, snacks, (fruit) soups, sweets and desserts.

## ✳ ALGAE

As just single-celled organisms, algae are among the oldest life forms on earth, dating back millions or even billions of years. And though it's safe to say that our current food chain has certainly evolved since the time of their origin, many of these primitive plant species still rank among the most nutritiously concentrated foods on earth. Scientists estimate there are over 30,000 species of algae in existence, each with varying degrees of benefits and nutrition (so perhaps don't run over to your fish tank to harvest the slimy green stuff just yet). Nonetheless, there are several single-cell superstars which offer truly exciting benefits—two of the most popular being spirulina and chlorella. These amazing chlorophyll-rich foods build the blood, alkalize the body (balance our pH), help build new cells, enhance the immune system, and so much more.

From an evolutionary standpoint, spirulina developed first. So primitive is this algae (which is of the blue-green variety), that it actually lacks a proper hard cellular wall—making it naturally easy for the body to access its nutrition. Exceptionally high in micronutrients, just three grams of spirulina contains more antioxidants and anti-inflammatory nutrients than five servings of vegetables.

It was chlorella, however, that became the first algae grown in large-scale production for food in the 1960s. Developing a few million years after spirulina, chlorella is a pure green algae that has a very hard cell wall. As a result, chlorella must go through a specialized manufacturing process that cracks the cell wall before it goes to market, or else it will simply pass through the body undigested.

It's no wonder that these foods are believed to be some of the most complete forms of food on the planet: both spirulina and chlorella contain a profoundly broad range of vitamins and minerals. Of particular interest is the presence of full-spectrum B vitamins (including B-12), which promotes natural energy. And in regards to macronutrients, algae are the most potent sources of complete protein of any food: chlorella is composed of 58 percent protein by weight, while spirulina boasts 60–70 percent protein (rank that next to chicken meat, for example, which is 25 percent protein). Touted benefits include reducing fatigue associated with PMS, relieving ulcers, and promoting bowel health.

But what algae are very best known for are their exceptional detoxification properties, due to their vast chlorophyll content. While all leafy vegetables contain chlorophyll, gram for gram none can even come close to matching the potency of these incredible algae. Most important (though not scientifically proven), many health practitioners now recognize that this high chlorophyll content has the ability to attract and flush out heavy metals from the body (such as those accrued through pesticides, environmental toxins, or radiation). Living in Los Angeles, I personally use algae on an almost daily basis to counterbalance the sometimes questionable air quality. And with modern medicine actively investigating their abilities to detoxify the body, improve the immune system, rebuild nerve tissue, improve mental function, fight against cancer, help in cases of osteoporosis and arthritis, and aid in weight loss, among many other uses, supplementing with these premium algae is almost a "must" in today's increasingly toxic world.

*Flavor notes:* Algae have a strong, sweetish, oceany taste that, admittedly, is not particularly exciting to most people. Luckily, this food is so ultra-concentrated in nutrition that even the smallest amount goes a very long way—making both spirulina and chlorella easy to sneak in unnoticed with other natural foods like fruit, savory sauces, and even sweets (especially chocolate). In general, most will agree that algae's flavor is generally best when "masked" by strong flavors.

*Recommended forms:* Powder (great for recipes) or tablets. Due to its higher chlorophyll content, I generally use chlorella over spirulina (as indicated in the recipes in this book), but both are indispensable foods and may be used interchangeably. Always buy "cracked cell" chlorella to ensure the nutrients are digestible.

*Use in:* Breakfasts, drinks and smoothies, snacks, salads and dressings, sweets and desserts.

## ✳ BERRIES (NORTH AMERICAN)

Most of North America's native berries cannot boast the same potency as some of their Latin American or overseas superberry cousins, such as maqui berries or goji berries. Nonetheless, almost all berries still rank among the world's most nutritious fruits. As one of humankind's very first food choices, berries function as one of the best antioxidant sources in the fruit kingdom—earning them a top spot in the ANDI rating system (see page 9) for their concentrated micronutrients (providing, for example, as much as a day's worth of vitamin C in just a cup) in conjunction with a low calorie content.

*Flavor notes:* Varying from sweet and fragrant (like raspberries), to tart with high tannins (like cranberries), edible North American berries are instinctively a prime food choice.

*Recommended forms:* Fresh or frozen strawberries, blueberries, cranberries, raspberries, or blackberries, as well as local heirloom varieties. Choose organically grown berries whenever possible, as conventionally grown berries unfortunately contain some of the highest levels of pesticides of all produce.

*Use in:* Breakfasts, drinks and smoothies, (fruit) soups, salads and dressings, sweets and desserts.

## ✖ CACAO

A prized food of the early Mayan empire, cacao is the raw, natural source of one of the most celebrated treats of all time: chocolate. And even more exciting, this unprocessed form of chocolate has so many fabulous, healthy attributes to offer that it ranks as one of the world's top superfoods.

Of course, our beloved chocolate doesn't grow in chocolate factories—it grows on tall cacao trees, which produce large, colorful, football-like pod fruits. Each pod is filled with large seeds known as "cacao beans," from which chocolate is made. If you apply a bit of pressure to a dried bean, it will break apart into small crunchy little pieces

Diversely colored cacao pods ripening on a tree.

(almost like mini chocolate chips) known as cacao nibs. And from here, all kinds of cacao products are created, including milled cacao powder, cacao butter, and cacao paste. Don't get confused between cacao and cocoa. The difference between the two is that while cacao is minimally processed at low temperatures, cocoa is toasted, roasted, or cooked in some manner that results in a much more heavily processed chocolate powder, lacking many of the original health benefits.

And those healthy benefits are huge. Cacao is one of the most antioxidant-rich foods in the world. To offer a little perspective on the magnitude of cacao's nutrition, let's compare it to an already well-known antioxidant-rich hero: blueberries. Blueberries provide a very respectable 6,000–9,000 ORAC units per 100 grams, depending on the plant source. Cacao earned an ORAC score of 95,000 units per 100 grams, ranking it as one of the top antioxidant foods ever tested. Additionally, cacao provides an excellent supply of minerals and is one of the best plant-based sources of magnesium— which, interestingly, supports a woman's intuition to consume chocolate during menses (magnesium is known to help relax muscles and reduce cramping). Cacao also contains particularly useful quantities of iron and calcium. Lastly, cacao contains several important phytochemicals (plant chemicals) and notable amounts of specific amino acids that support mood-elevating brain chemistry. It goes without saying, cacao is a feel-good food all around, and if you like chocolate, you are going adore cacao. It's a fabulous, healthy upgrade from cocoa or conventional chocolate, and provides a pleasurable energy boost.

*Flavor notes:* Cacao tastes like strong, unsweetened chocolate. It is less aromatic and slightly milder in flavor than (roasted) cocoa, and benefits greatly when paired with a small amount of mesquite powder, carob powder, dates, or other food that contains caramel undertones that help round out and strengthen its flavor.

*Recommended forms:* Cacao beans, cacao nibs, cacao powder, cacao butter, or cacao paste. (The recipes in this book utilize cacao powder, cacao nibs, and cacao butter only.) Please note that cacao butter, while a healthier source of saturated fat than animal-derived saturated fats, contains almost no nutritional value (other than fat) on its own. Although used in a few dessert recipes in this book, this cacao product is not marked as (nor should be considered) a superfood ingredient. On the reverse end of the spectrum, cacao powder is the best superfood source of cacao; as it has had most of its fat ("butter") extracted, it is the most condensed in benefits.

*Use in:* Breakfasts, drinks and smoothies, snacks, sweets and desserts. Best used in raw food recipes.

## ✳ CAMU CAMU BERRY

Some people call it camu camu, other people just call it camu, but either way this is quite the beneficial berry. Camu grows as a small shrub-like tree in hot and damp tropical climates, such as the low-lying areas of the Peruvian Amazon. The berry itself is a small, reddish-purple, cherry-like fruit that's traditionally harvested by canoes during the flooding season, much like cranberries.

Camu has long been used by native peoples in Amazonian folk medicine, but it's really only been popularized in Western culture within the last

Camu camu berries growing in the Amazon.

One last note: you don't ever want to heat camu, as heat will destroy the sensitive vitamin C content—which is what we're after in the first place! Therefore, I like to use camu in a lot of food preparations that don't require cooking.

*Flavor notes:* Even though camu is a berry, it's not exactly the kind of sweet berry you'd get excited about topping a fruit bowl with. Camu is extremely tart—even more so than a cranberry—which is a by-product of the copious amounts of vitamin C, a naturally bitter substance. Luckily, the fruit is so condensed in nutrition you can get away with putting as little as a quarter of a teaspoon of camu into a recipe and still receive huge benefits. So, admittedly, while this isn't your go-to fruit for flavor enhancement, it is extremely easy to sneak in with other foods and get all that extra premium vitamin C.

*Recommended forms:* Organic, freeze-dried camu powder is an ideal form because of its purity, digestibility, and overall flexibility in recipes.

*Use in:* Breakfasts, drinks and smoothies, sides, snacks, (fruit) soups, salads and dressings, entrées, sweets and desserts. Best used in raw food recipes.

## ❋ CHIA SEED

Yes, these are the same seeds used for growing the notorious "Chia Pet." Had I only known better back in the day, I would have had an extra place to grab a free meal in addition to having a kitschy desk ornament.

Thankfully, the Chia Pet does not get credit for the first use of chia seeds. Chia has actually been

century. The fresh fruit itself is physically composed of 2–3 percent pure vitamin C by weight, which translates to about 30–60 times more vitamin C than an orange! Just one tiny teaspoon of powdered camu berry contains a whopping 1,180 percent RDA vitamin C content. Plus, they also contain a broad range of naturally occurring antioxidants, phytochemicals, amino acids, and vitamins and minerals, such as beta carotene and potassium. The presence of all these intrinsically symbiotic substances in a whole food form means the human body is able to assimilate and utilize these impressive vitamins much more easily than from synthetic pills or isolated forms of vitamin C. Essentially, camu is nature's vitamin C supplement . . . with some great extra benefits thrown in.

used for thousands of years—it was once a staple food source among the Aztecs, Incas, and Mayans, who used it to increase strength and maintain stamina during long journeys. Their dependence upon chia makes a lot of sense: even though chia is tiny—smaller than a sesame seed—it is unbelievably packed with nutrients that promote long-lasting energy.

Chia is similar in nutrition to another better-known superfood: flaxseed. Both are revered as exceptional plant-based sources of important omega-3 fatty acids, which—aside from balancing the ratio of EFAs (Essential Fatty Acids) within our naturally high omega-6 diet—also support increased mental function, lowered inflammation, cardiovascular health, and immune system support. One distinct advantage chia has over flax is an abundance of antioxidants that are not only beneficial, but also help keep all its healthy fats from oxidizing. Beyond being a source of easily digestible protein, chia contains a wealth of important minerals, especially calcium and iron. Chia seeds are also a tremendous source of fiber: just one tablespoon provides over a quarter of our daily requirements for fiber.

Chia is not only incredible from a nutrition standpoint, it's also an unusual and fun food to use in the kitchen. Chia's high fiber content contains a high amount of mucilage, which means the chia absorbs water very easily and will actually "plump up" when combined with liquid, forming a kind of "gel" layer around each seed. A chia seed can absorb about nine times its weight in water, which means that once it is digested, it expands in the stomach and creates a sensation of fullness. It's no wonder that many people consider chia an exceptional food for dieting and weight loss.

*Flavor notes:* Raw chia seed tastes like almost nothing at all, which makes it a breeze to add into recipes. Think of chia as more of a textural component: used as a slightly crunchy topping, or as a binding agent or thickener when soaked and allowed to gel.

*Recommended forms:* Black or white whole chia seed is excellent (both have essentially the same nutritional properties; black chia seed is usually less expensive). Also available is sprouted chia seed powder, which takes advantage of the nutritional boost that happens whenever a seed sprouts. In this form, the chia seeds are gently re-dried after having sprouted, then milled into a fine powder. The result serves as an undetectable nutritious addition to flours, or can be hydrated with water to act as a binder/healthy egg substitute in baking.

*Use in:* Breakfasts, drinks and smoothies, sides, snacks, soups, salads and dressings, entrées, sweets and desserts. Ground chia powder is especially useful in baking.

## ✳ FLAXSEED

A shiny brown seed that is slightly larger then a sesame seed, flax originated in Mesopotamia and has been utilized since the Stone Age. Like chia, flaxseed is known for its beneficial essential fatty acid (EFA) profile (omega-3, -6, and -9). Though flax may not have the same variety or quantity of antioxidants that chia offers, it does contain an excellent supply of valuable lignans—a class of phytochemicals (with antioxidant properties) known to help balance hormone levels. Along with a notable amount of protein, flaxseed is also exceptionally high in fiber and is often used to promote regularity. Like chia seeds, flax also contains a notable amount of mucilage, allowing the flax to absorb moisture easily, acting as an ideal thickener and binder.

It should be noted that while flaxseed is quite toothsome in its whole form, to enjoy its nutritional attributes the seeds must be ground in order for the body to fully digest them. Otherwise, the whole flaxseeds will simply pass through the body.

Who knew flaxseed powder could be sold under so many names? You'll likely come across flaxseed powder, flaxseed meal, powdered flax, ground flax, milled flax . . . and they're all virtually the same thing. You can make your own, too: just purchase whole flaxseeds and grind them up fresh using a coffee or spice grinder. Then, you can call it whatever you want!

*Flavor notes:* Raw flaxseed has a pleasant, mild, nutty flavor that quickly slips into the background when combined with other nuts or seeds. When toasted, the nuttiness is enhanced. Exposure to very high heat will induce a pronounced oily flavor and should be avoided.

*Recommended forms:* Many people like to buy raw whole brown or golden flaxseed and freshly grind it using a coffee grinder, but pre-ground flax may be used as well (and kept refrigerated to protect its sensitive EFAs). Another exceptional form is a sprouted flaxseed powder produced by Navitas Naturals (page 228). The process of germination actually changes the nutrient composition of the flaxseed, and maximizes the body's ability to digest and absorb its nutritional benefits. It also results in a larger number of enzymes, vitamins, and minerals, and its finely milled powder form allows it to blend seamlessly into recipes of all kinds. Because of its increased nutrition, I highly recommend using this sprouted form, if possible, wherever a recipe calls for "flaxseed powder." Flax oil is also available, and can be used as an "EFA Oil" source (see page 40 for EFA oils). Though flax oil has many healthy benefits, it is not considered a superfood due to its low nutrient density.

*Use in:* Breakfasts, drinks and smoothies, sides, snacks, soups, salads and dressings, entrées, sweets and desserts. Flaxseed powder can also be used as a partial flour substitute, or used as a binder/egg substitute in baking when combined with a little liquid (see page 57 for more on this technique).

## ✺ GOLDENBERRY

If you haven't heard of a goldenberry before, perhaps you're familiar with one of its other dozens of names, such as cape gooseberry, incan berry, poha berry, or husk cherry. Whatever name you choose to call it, this amazing fruit comes from a bush commonly known as the "Chinese Lantern," whose paper-like husk flowers (resembling little lanterns) cradle a precious, golden, cherry-like fruit on the inside. These fruits—goldenberries—provide remarkable levels of antioxidants (such as carotenes and bioflavonoids), as well as good amounts of vitamin A, vitamin C, protein, and phosphorus. High levels of bioflavonoids have been linked to reducing inflammation and strengthening the immune system. In addition, goldenberries are naturally lower in sugar than many other fruits.

*Flavor notes:* Remarkable is the best way to describe the flavor of the goldenberry. These berries have a complex sweet-sour flavor with a citrus-like

Sun-dried goldenberries are an excellent snack food.

## ✳ GOJI BERRY

Goji, an English contraction of the Mandarin name, *gouqi* (pronounced "goo-chee"), meaning wolfberry, is among the most popular superfoods available, and for good reason. Goji berries have a long history of use in Chinese medicine, extending back thousands of years, as a secret to longevity and strengthening the immune system. Today, clinical trials have confirmed the goji is indeed one of the most powerful superfoods known, with an exceptional balance of all macronutrients (protein, carbohydrates, fat, and even soluble fiber). Goji berries feature eighteen amino acids (including all eight essential amino acids), which are 10 percent of the fruit's composition. Impressive in the micronutrient department as well, goji berries are a phenomenal source of antioxidants, including carotenoids like beta carotene, lutein, zeaxanthin and lycopene (rarely found in berries). And this wonder of nature doesn't stop there! Goji berries also contain over twenty vitamins and trace minerals like vitamin C, zinc, riboflavin (Vitamin B-2), and iron.

quality that truly takes your taste buds for a ride. Frankly, my favorite way to enjoy them is just on their own, taking my time with each one, and experiencing the full spectrum of their flavor.

*Recommended forms:* Goldenberries don't last very long after they've been picked, making finding them fresh a rarity. Luckily, goldenberries are increasingly available in a sun-dried form. Better still, their flavor is greatly enhanced by drying them in this fashion. Look for sun-dried goldenberries in natural food stores or online.

*Use in:* Breakfasts, drinks and smoothies, sides, snacks, salads and dressings, sweets and desserts.

*Flavor notes:* Goji berries have a distinct sweet flavor that is a cross between a cranberry, cherry, and tomato.

*Recommended forms:* Dried goji berries are by far the most widely available form. Goji berry powder, juice, and fresh-frozen goji berries are other useful forms now available.

*Use in:* Breakfasts, drinks and smoothies, sides, snacks, salads and dressings, entrées, sweets and desserts.

## ✳ GRASSES

Don't let the word "grass" fool you: supergrasses like wheatgrass, kamut grass, and barley grass are no ordinary plants. Admittedly, they sound pretty humble: they are simply sprouts that grow from planting grains like wheat or barley. Yet their inspiring benefits have made them quite famous.

While there are records of ancient Egyptians using wheatgrass for cleansing and vitality purposes over 5,000 years ago, and references to Roman gladiators using barley grass for stamina, it wasn't until the 1930s that scientists began to closely study the phenomenal benefits of these "supergrasses." Soon after, revolutionary health practitioners began to include grasses as a key ingredient in their thera-peutic programs, treating health problems ranging from chronic fatigue to cancer. Hence, wheatgrass juice (and later, other grass juices as well) became our first "official" modern-day, Western-world superfood. Grasses have been used ever since as a star ingredient in health conscious lifestyles—extolled for generating healthy energy, neutralizing toxins, and delaying aging.

Their popularity is easy to understand. With a 70 percent chlorophyll composition, supergrasses rank amongst the richest sources of chlorophyll known, making them exceptionally alkaline-forming and supportive of a healthy pH balance. Research has shown that along with offering an abundance of live enzymes, these special greens also contain about eighty naturally occurring nutrients—including

Though wheatgrass is available in several forms, the powder is the most palatable and the easiest to sneak into recipes.

every known vitamin and amino acid. Needless to say, you'd have to eat a lot of vegetables to match something as powerful as that.

**Note:** Generally speaking, grasses are gluten-free despite their grain origin—gluten resides in the proteins inside the grain seed, not in the grass foliage.

*Flavor notes:* Sweet and indeed grassy, wheatgrass, kamut grass, and barley grass are much bolder in flavor when consumed fresh, while distinctly more mild (and almost undetectable) when used in a freeze-dried powder form.

*Recommended forms:* Freshly juiced grasses are exceptional, but the one snag with this route is the grasses must be enjoyed very fresh—literally within minutes of being juiced—or else they quickly lose much of their nutritional potency. Therefore, my form of choice is actually a freeze-dried powder. Outside of simply being very convenient (you just mix a little powder with water or juice and you've got instant wheatgrass), this highly concentrated form holds the live enzymes and nutrients that are present when the grass is freshly juiced in a protective suspension. When exposed to moisture (by adding liquid), the nutrients are reactivated, ensuring you're able to take advantage of all the delicate benefits inside. A freeze-dried powder is rewardingly easy to sneak into foods of all kind, and while the recipes in this book specify freeze-dried wheatgrass powder as an ingredient (see the Ingredient Resources Guide, page 228, for a quality source), kamut and/or barley grass may certainly be substituted.

*Use in:* Breakfasts, drinks and smoothies, snacks, soups, entrées, sweets and desserts.

## ✳ GREEN LEAFY VEGETABLES

I imagine it comes as a shock to no one that green leafy vegetables are an essential part of a healthy diet. But green vegetables prove their worth as bona fide superfoods due to the phenomenal wealth of nutrition they have to offer. In fact, the ANDI system (which sadly does not measure many of the lesser-known superfoods included in this pantry list; see page 9) ranks green vegetables as the very healthiest of all the foods by a long shot. Consider kale, which boasts a cool 1,000 ANDI score (on a scale of 1–1,000)! What this implies is that green leafy vegetables are the epitome of efficient eating: high quality nutrition at a low calorie cost. Exceptionally high in chlorophyll, these great greens also contain a wealth of both vitamins and minerals, amino acids (protein), and fiber. If there's one superfood I believe trumps all others in terms of overall value and balance, it's green leafy vegetables. Viva la green!

**Note:** Leafy culinary herbs are undoubtedly included in this superfood category. In fact, many—parsley and oregano, for example—are considered more than just nutritious foods, but actually medicinal agents as well. Although herbs clearly cannot be used in the same abundance as green vegetables due to their pungent flavors, including these fresh, natural flavor enhancers whenever possible is an instant way to add health-giving nutrients to a dish.

*Flavor notes:* Each vegetable has its own flavor profile—some mild, some bitter, some salty, some spicy—and it's awesome to experience the subtle differences between varieties of leaves. Try a different green at the market each week and explore the enjoyable nuances of nature's finest vegetables.

*Recommended forms:* There's hardly an edible green leafy vegetable that isn't recommended, but as a rule of thumb, the darker the green, the more beneficial the food. Some greens that score at the top of the nutrient density spectrum include collard greens, kale, watercress, bok choy, spinach, broccoli, cabbage, brussels sprouts, swiss chard, arugula, and dark lettuces. Fresh is always best, but frozen vegetables are a convenient option as well. Powdered green blends (usually sold in the supplement section of markets) provide an instant and efficient green boost, and are good to have on hand for times when eating "green" is not feasible. Excellent-choice fresh green herbs include parsley, cilantro, basil, oregano, sage, and many more—the perfect garden pot or window-sill planter additions.

*Use in:* Drinks and smoothies, sides, snacks, soups, salads and dressings, entrées.

## ✳ HEMP SEED

It's hard to pick favorite superfoods—much like picking a favorite child—but hemp seeds might just rank on my top five list. Aside from simply being a delicious and effortless seed to use, hemp offers extraordinary nutrition. Hemp has a recorded history of use dating back over 12,000 years, and was actually one of the very first crops planted in the colony of Jamestown before the United States was even a country. (Its uses were so extensive that in 1619 it was, in fact, mandatory that farmers grow it.) A profoundly sustainable plant, the oil of the seed is composed of valuable essential fatty acids in a particularly well-balanced ratio (including heart-healthy omega-3s). Hemp's high saturation of

protein is of a premium quality, as well—an easily digestible, plant-based, complete protein boasting all essential amino acids. Hemp also offers a wide range of minerals, especially iron, potassium, zinc, and magnesium. Better still, hemp is an excellent source of fiber, and is one of the few alkaline-forming seeds in nature, due to the small green filament on the inside of the kernel. Of course, hemp's great taste makes all this nutrition a pleasure to enjoy, earning hemp seed the status of a true "everyday" superfood.

*Flavor notes:* Soft, raw, hulled hemp seeds taste similar to sunflower seeds, and can be used as a rich nutty addition to recipes. Roasted hemp seeds have a much more pronounced nutty, almond-like flavor. Hemp protein provides an earthy and sometimes mildly grassy flavor, as it is often ground with the hemp husk still on. Deep green hemp oil is a rich and nutty gourmet oil, ideal for low-heat applications.

*Recommended forms:* Raw hemp seeds, roasted hemp seeds, hemp protein powder/flour, and hemp oil. Use the raw form of hemp seeds for the recipes in this book. Hemp milk can also be obtained at health food markets, or, better yet, made from scratch (page 224). Please note that while hemp oil is of "superfood origin" and has many healthy benefits, it is not a superfood ingredient per se, due to its low nutrient density. Rather, consider hemp oil a healthy pantry staple (as described in the EFA Oils section, page 40). It is certainly one of the healthiest oil choices available.

*Use in:* Breakfasts, drinks and smoothies, sides, snacks, soups, salads and dressings, entrées, sweets and desserts.

## ✳ MACA

A radish-like root, maca is indigenous to the highlands of the Peruvian Andes, where it has been used medicinally for thousands of years. Traditionally, Incan warriors depended upon maca to increase both strength and stamina during their long battles. Today, maca is best known for offering healthy energy, regulating stress, and supporting the adrenal glands, as well as promoting sexual health and balancing hormones.

Key to understanding the exceptional power of maca is its placement within a rare class of plants called "adaptogens" (only about 1 in 4,000 plants contains adaptogenic properties). Being an adaptogen means that, when consumed, this amazing root can actually "adapt" and adjust to combat the different types of stresses that are put on the body. Remarkably, maca strengthens and balances the body's systems—providing long-lasting energy and combating fatigue—without being a stimulant.

Maca also contains around sixty phytonutrients, including abundant minerals, amino acids, and a noteworthy quantity of beneficial plant sterols, which have been shown to help block cholesterol absorption.

*Flavor notes:* Maca offers a strong aroma and a complex, earthy, slightly sweet, nutty flavor—with just a hint of butterscotch. Its unusual taste may be pulled in both sweet and savory directions, and many find it strangely addictive.

*Recommended forms:* Either a raw or gelatinized (concentrated) whole root powder is ideal for recipes and long-term storage. I prefer the milder flavor and the higher potency of the gelatinized version.

*Use in:* Breakfasts, drinks and smoothies, sides, soups, entrées, sweets and desserts.

## ✳ MAQUI BERRY

The Mapuche Indians of Chile include deep purple maqui berries as a staple element of their diet . . . and also happen to be amongst the longest-living people in the world. Coincidence? A quick look at maqui's nutrition and you're likely to decide no. At the time of this writing, maqui berries are the single highest (known) antioxidant fruit in the world, with up to 9,200 ORAC units per gram—almost double the antioxidant activity of acai berries. In particular, maqui berries have a strong concentration of two antioxidants (of the flavonoid variety), known as polyphenols and anthocyanins, which repair and protect DNA. Studies have also shown that berries with anthocyanins are particularly beneficial in reducing oxidative stress associated with aging, as well as improving brain function. Add in quality amounts of vitamin C, minerals, as well as several anti-inflammatory compounds, and it's clear maqui is a tremendously exciting food for health and anti-aging.

*Flavor notes:* Maqui berries have a very mellow berry flavor, similar to a mild, less-sweet blueberry. Much stronger is maqui's enchanting purple hue that can be used as a natural coloring agent when added to pale foods. So intense and beautiful is maqui's color (a signal of its potent antioxidants), that native Mapuche cultures often use maqui as an indigo dye.

*Recommended forms:* Aside from fresh berries (not available in North America), the most active and pure form of maqui is a freeze-dried powder. This way, the berry is never exposed to high temperatures, enabling its maximum nutrients to be sustained for consumption.

*Use in:* Breakfasts, drinks and smoothies, sides, snacks, soups, salads and dressings, entrées, sweets and desserts.

## ✳ MULBERRY

Mulberries may taste like a normal, deliciously sweet berry, but their unique set of benefits significantly surpasses that of more commonly known berries, such as blueberries or cranberries (which, as we've discussed, are wonderful to begin with). Considered a top "anti-aging" superfood, mulberries contain a particularly high concentration of resveratrol—an antioxidant compound that combats free-radical damage, fights inflammation, and provides protection against some of the most prevalent degenerative diseases of our time: Alzheimer's, some forms of cancer, and Parkinson's disease. Recent studies have shown that regular consumption of this special antioxidant also helps promote heart health and longevity. Resveratrol is not found in many foods, making mulberries' concentration of this antioxidant a unique and sought-after benefit.

Mulberries are also one of the few fruits to be considered a protein source, boasting a respectable 3 grams of protein per ounce. In addition, they are an excellent source of iron, calcium, vitamin C, and fiber.

*Flavor notes:* Fresh mulberries are sweet, but often a little bland. It's dried mulberries that offer

Sun-dried white Turkish mulberries.

the real big-time delicious flavor. These sun-dried fruits taste like a sweet cross between raisins and vanilla. Their flavor has always reminded me a bit of vanilla cake.

*Recommended forms:* Sun-dried mulberries, white or red, for flavor and shelf life. Fresh mulberries are wonderful to enjoy as well, but are usually confined to their local growing areas during a very short harvesting season (they do not ship well).

*Use in:* Breakfasts, drinks and smoothies, snacks, salads and dressings, sweets and desserts.

## ✳ POMEGRANATE

With cultivation dating back to prehistoric ages and a long history of both medicinal and culinary uses, the pomegranate is a well-established superfood. Pomegranates contain a broad spectrum of vitamins and minerals, especially vitamin C and potassium. They are also a powerful source of antioxidants like phytoestrogens and polyphenols, and are packed with anti-inflammatory essential amino acids. Among the most important effects of the pomegranate is the fruit's incredible ability to inhibit free radicals (a biological phenomenon which contributes to disease and aging). Remarkably, the polyphenols in pomegranates have been found to inhibit estrogen synthesis—with the oil from the pomegranate seed now proven effective against the proliferation of breast cancer cells in vitro. Separate scientific studies have also shown pomegranate to be a proactive food in lowering cholesterol and blood pressure.

*Flavor Notes:* Pomegranate offers a flavorful, tart, and sweet fruity taste at a low sugar cost. If whole seeds are used, there is also a mild nutty influence from the kernel.

*Recommended sources:* Fresh fruit, bottled or fresh-pressed juice (check the ingredients to ensure no sugar has been added), and freeze-dried powder (for a very saturated flavor and long shelf life).

*Use in:* Breakfasts, drinks and smoothies, salads and dressings, entrées, sweets and desserts.

## ✳ QUINOA

Between its addictively delicious, mildly nutty flavor, and a delightfully fluffy texture that shouts "comfort food," it's not a great mystery why quinoa is instantly embraced by almost every person who tries it. Tiny in size (about the size of amaranth or millet), quinoa is usually treated like a grain or starch, cooking up just like rice or pasta in a fraction of the time. Although quinoa acts convincingly grain-like, it's actually the nutritious seed of a vegetable that's a closer relative to spinach, which means it's also gluten-free. Often advertised as an "ancient grain," quinoa is native to South America, where it was once a staple food of the Incas, and has been cultivated for over 3,000 years.

Quinoa is most famous for an impressive protein content—around 11 grams per half cup (uncooked)—that happens to boast all eight essential amino acids. Additionally, quinoa provides many minerals, such as magnesium, potassium, and zinc. It even includes some vitamins too, like skin and hair-rejuvenating vitamin E, plus many of the energy-giving B vitamins. I find quinoa to be one of the most all-purpose superfoods available because it does such a delicious job of functioning as the starchy component we crave in our food, while providing truly solid nutrition.

*Flavor notes:* Quinoa's flavor is a deliciously familiar cross between pasta and rice, with just a hint of nuttiness. In its natural state, quinoa is coated with a bitter substance called saponin, which acts as the plant's self-produced organic pesticide. The saponins are easily washed away by rinsing the seeds before cooking. Quickly dry-toasting the quinoa for a minute or two in a frying pan (before cooking in boiling water) will increase the nut-like flavor—an optional but rewarding extra step.

*Recommended forms:* Whole grain quinoa is the most commonly used form of quinoa, which is often available in bulk. There are literally hundreds of quinoa varieties: white is the most common, red and black types of quinoa offer extra antioxidants and visual appeal, and all taste virtually identical. Additionally, 100 percent quinoa flour makes a nutritious baking ingredient, though it does lend a slightly bitter taste and is best used in small quantities in recipes with stronger flavors. New on the market is quinoa pasta, which is made using quinoa flour in conjunction with another mild gluten-free flour (the perfect example of a traditionally empty-calorie food made beneficial through the use of superfood ingredients). And lastly, delicious quinoa flakes (which are essentially a flat-rolled quinoa—think rolled oats) are a fantastic form of this superfood. The flakes cook almost instantly and work amazingly well as a cross between an oatmeal-type ingredient and a bread crumb.

*Use in:* Breakfasts, sides, snacks, soups, entrées.

## ✴ SACHA INCHI

With *sacha* meaning "looks like" and *inchi* meaning "peanut/nut," the exotic Amazonian sacha inchi seed is not much of an enigma. Enjoyed for centuries since pre-Incan civilizations (where ceramics have been recovered with imprints of sacha inchi seeds), these jungle seeds are as large as a nut—about two-thirds the size of an almond—and have an indulgent richness about them. Sacha inchi is abundant in easily digestible protein and is an excellent source of dietary fiber. Most exciting, however, is that these special seeds are the single highest known source of healthy, plant-based, omega-3 fats on the planet—with over thirteen times more omega-3s than salmon, ounce for ounce. Sacha inchi is also a particularly good source of tryptophan—the "good mood"

amino acid that turkey is famous for (sacha inchi contains eight times more tryptophan than turkey, ounce for ounce). And on top of all that, it boasts a useful mineral and antioxidant collection that includes iodine, vitamin A, and vitamin E. Personally, I can't help but think of these seeds as the "beauty seeds," as their nutrients are so good for getting a healthy glow on.

*Flavor notes:* True to the literal translation of their name, these seeds really do taste similar to a peanut, yet have a distinctly umami/savory taste component . . . one that makes me instinctually hungry for some any time someone even mentions their name. Sacha inchi are crunchy, filling, and go well with either sweet or savory foods.

*Recommended forms:* In North America, these seeds are sold in a lightly roasted, whole seed form (they are very perishable when raw, and are not currently available this way in North America). Sacha inchi oil is also available, which makes a beneficial salad dressing oil, and is best used unheated. (Please note that sacha inchi oil is considered a healthy pantry item but not a true superfood ingredient, due to a low overall nutrient density ratio).

*Use in:* Breakfasts, sides, snacks, soups, salads and dressings, entrées, sweets and desserts.

## ✴ SEA BUCKTHORN

Indeed, sea buckthorn may sound like a strange offering from the ocean, but it is actually a small orange berry that grows in clusters on thorny bushes or spindly trees. This interesting berry likely acquired its quirky name from its preference to grow along the dry sand dunes hugging English coastlines (do note that sea buckthorn is not the same species as "regular" buckthorn). Tart, oily, and difficult to harvest, sea buckthorn may not seem like an eager berry-picker's first choice, yet sea buckthorn has long enjoyed celebrity as a prized food due to its special medicinal offerings. Traditionally found along the Atlantic coastlines and sandy regions of many European and Asian countries (each offering its own regional name variation for the berry), sea buckthorn is best known for rejuvenating the skin and has also been found to enhance cardiovascular, digestive, and liver health. In fact, records of sea buckthorn used as an important herbal remedy can be found in ancient Greek texts, as well as in Tibetan medical documents as far back as the Tang Dynasty (618–907 AD).

Modern nutritional analysis of sea buckthorn confirms the berry as an impressive skin-healing food, with several nutritional factors to credit. As a powerful source of vitamin C and many other vitamins, plus free-radical–scavenging polyphones and carotenoids, sea buckthorn acts as a natural anti-aging agent that helps fight inflammation. Also impressive are its quantity and array of omega fats, including omega-3, omega-6, omega-9, and even the especially rare omega-7, which promotes healthy skin, hair, and nails through tissue recovery and healing, among many other benefits. Due to its unique and valuable nutritional composition, sea buckthorn remains a top-tier medicinal superfood, and a continual subject of scientific interest.

*Flavor notes:* Often described as sour, tart, and oily, sea buckthorn usually does not earn high taste-test marks all by itself. Yet its flavor is not harsh and, combined with other foods, can provide a complex, citrus-like "zing" that is intriguing and complemented by sugars and sweet juices, as well as savory fats like avocado.

*Recommended Forms:* Sea buckthorn is often sold as a concentrated oil to condense its omega benefits. It is often used topically on the skin in this form. For culinary purposes, however, a pure sea buckthorn juice is best—it provides the berry's largest spectrum of benefits and flavor, and is the easiest to incorporate into recipes.

*Use in:* Drinks and smoothies, salads and dressings, soups, sweets and desserts. Best used in low heat or raw food recipes.

## ⚜ SEA VEGETABLES

Ocean water is profoundly high in minerals, and the plants that live beneath the sea function as absorbent sponges for all these important nutrients. Sea vegetables (sometimes referred to as seaweeds) are among the oldest living species on earth, and have been consumed in Asian cultures for thousands of years (dating back to at least 3000 BC in China). But like so many superfoods, it's only recently that sea vegetables are finding their way into mainstream Western cuisine. Frankly, their rising popularity couldn't have come at a better time; with mineral depletion in farm soil rapidly on the rise, sea vegetables offer a condensed replenishment of lost dietary minerals, supplying the nutrition our bodies need and crave.

Sea greens are also one of nature's top sources of vegetable protein, and provide an abundance of beta carotene, chlorophyll, enzymes, amino acids, fiber, and other micronutrients. Their salty taste isn't "just salt" either—it's a mark of their high mineral composition, including a balanced spectrum of sodium, potassium, calcium, magnesium, phosphorus, and numerous trace minerals. Vitamins are plentiful too, especially vitamins K, A, D, E, and the B family. In fact, sea vegetables provide one of the few plant-based sources of vitamin B-12. Just think of sea vegetables as land vegetables, except with about ten to twenty times the micronutrients, and the tremendous potential to heal, detoxify, nourish, and energize.

**Note:** Because sea vegetables act like a filter to the ocean water in which they grow, a clean source of these foods is of the utmost importance to ensure purity. Reputable sources can be found in the Ingredient Resources Guide (page 228).

*Flavor notes:* The Japanese consider sea vegetables to be one of the few foods in the "umami" flavor category (otherwise known as the "fifth flavor"), which is often defined as savory or mouthwatering. Each sea vegetable has a distinctively different taste—some are sweet, some fishy, some exceptionally salty, others almost meaty.

*Recommended forms:* Usually sold dried, all commercial sea vegetables from certified clean waters are beneficial. Some of the most useful in the kitchen include dulse (both flakes and strips), kelp (especially powder), nori sheets, wakame (sometimes sold as alaria), and gelatin-like agar agar. There are many more varieties, so once you are comfortable with the above "basics," feel free to branch out!

*Use in:* Sides, snacks, soups, salads and dressings, entrées.

## ✺ SPROUTS

Sprouts are baby plants and vegetables, but in many ways the sprout stage of a plant is its nutritional prime. The process of germination dramatically improves the nutritional profile of the dormant seed—multiplying the seed's nutritional benefit anywhere from 300 to 1,200 percent! As a result, sprouts are an incredibly nutrient-dense food, boasting copious amounts of enzymes, vitamins, minerals, chlorophyll, antioxidants, and even protein.

Many sprouts reign nutritionally supreme when compared to their corresponding adult plant, too. Take radishes for example: 100 mg of radish sprouts contain almost twice the calcium and thirty-nine times the vitamin A of an equal amount of mature radish. Sprouts are condensed nutrition at its finest, and provide a fabulous, fresh superfood that can be bought at stores or easily grown at home for literally pennies a day on a kitchen countertop.

*Flavor notes:* Like vegetables, sprouts can range in flavor from lightly "green" tasting to spicy. Clover sprouts are among the most innocuous, while radish sprouts bring a nice bite to a dish. One personal favorite is onion sprouts, which taste like mild onions—excellent in salads or sandwiches.

*Recommended forms:* All sprouts contain benefits; some especially savory ones include clover, alfalfa, sunflower, radish, broccoli, onion, mung bean, and pea shoots. Microgreens—the baby leaves of vegetables like beets, arugula, cabbage, etc.—are an excellent choice when available, as they are very mild in flavor and

Fresh sprouts and microgreens are available in many stores and farmers' markets, and can be homegrown, too.

instantly enhance the presentation of a dish. Sprouted grains and legumes can be delicious, chewy additions to foods as well; some of the more popular varieties include lentils, wheat berries, rye, and buckwheat. Flours made from sprouted seeds and grains are sometimes available too, like sprouted flax powder and sprouted chia powder (Ingredient Resources Guide, page 228).

*Use in:* Breakfasts, sides, snacks, salads and dressings, entrées. Sprouted seed flours/powders may be used as a partial flour substitute. Fresh sprouts should primarily be used raw due to their physical delicacy and sensitive nutrients.

## ✳ YACON

Many people think that yacon is a fruit—probably because it has a sweet and smoky apple-like flavor, and can be eaten as a whole food or used as a sweetener. But instead, yacon is in fact a tuber that grows in the ground beneath a low-lying plant. Native to South America, yacon has been cultivated as long ago as 1200 BC! Many people in the Andes still use the yacon plant extensively in medicine as well as in their traditional cuisine, and it has proven especially important as a healthy sweetener, improving the quality of life for many people suffering from symptoms of diabetes.

A yacon flower.

the body. Even more exciting, FOS promote healthy probiotics, which contribute to better digestion and colon health. With these benefits, it's easy to understand why it's a long-time favorite South American superfood.

*Flavor notes:* Both fresh and dried yacon are reminiscent of a mild apple with tea-like flavor undertones. The syrup is like a light, fruity molasses.

*Recommended forms:* Outside of South America where yacon can be found fresh, the root is most readily available in the form of dried yacon slices and yacon syrup. Although yacon syrup is among the healthiest sweeteners around, the syrup is not a superfood by itself (it is still a concentrated sugar).

Yacon's greatest attribute is a high content of inulin, a complex sugar that breaks down slowly into fructo-oligosaccharides (also known as FOS). So, although yacon tastes sweet, the sugar from the inulin is not digestible and simply passes through

*Use in:* Breakfasts, drinks and smoothies, sides, snacks, soups, salads and dressings, entrées, sweets and desserts.

# HEALTHY PANTRY STAPLES

Looking only at the effects of any one single food isn't going to give us the "big-picture health" we're after. So, although many plant foods don't make the nutrient-density cut of "superfood status," that doesn't mean they are without benefit. (Most whole foods have a welcome place within the superfood kitchen.) Healthy pantry staples include substitutions for less-desired counterparts or simple smart-choice ingredients that add flavor and balance. Each pantry staple listed here serves as an ideal complement to a superfood-rich diet.

## AGAVE NECTAR

Extracted from the agave cactus, this sweet syrup has proven especially valuable to the diabetic community because of its low glycemic index (due to a naturally high fructose content, which does not require insulin to break down and is readily metabolized). Although it should only be used sparingly due to its concentrated sugars, its potent sweetening ability and lack of detectable flavor make it a very efficient sweetener in certain applications. You can get away with using much less agave than other sweeteners, which often reduces the overall sugar content of a recipe. I like to use small amounts of it in conjunction with other sweeteners, such as sugar-free stevia (page 44).

## COCONUT OIL

Coconut oil is nature's version of butter: It has a satiating richness that seems to make everything it's added to a little bit more delicious. Yet coconut oil isn't just another pretty taste—it also comes with a multitude of smart benefits. Considered a "healthy" saturated fat source (due to being a plant-based oil), it has no cholesterol (the opposite of animal-derived saturated fats), and actually helps metabolize other beneficial fats, such as omega-3s.

Coconut oil also features medium-chain fatty acids (MCFAs, which promote long-lasting energy, increased metabolic rates, and even anti-bacterial, anti-viral, and anti-fungal activity). And since saturated fats are naturally resistant to oxidation, coconut oil remains a stable oil at a much higher temperature than most oils, making it ideal to cook with. For both its exceptional taste and healthy benefits, coconut oil is undoubtedly my go-to oil for any kind of high-heat application, and I consider it a must-have in any good natural food pantry.

Just like varieties of olive oils, different brands of coconut oil will vary in coconut-flavor intensity—some are mild and buttery, others richly tropical. Generally speaking, the cold-processed or centrifuge-extracted varieties will offer a milder coconut aroma and flavor, whereas expeller-pressed brands will be more intensely aromatic. I usually opt for the cold-pressed variety, as it's the most flexible flavor-wise due to its cleaner taste.

**Note:** Coconut oil is usually found in a white solid state that may be easily melted (if desired) into a clear liquid simply by heating the oil above 75° F.

## COCONUT (PALM) SUGAR

A healthier alternative to cane sugar, coconut sugar (sometimes sold as palm sugar) is made from the crystallized nectar of the cococunt tree blossoms. It has half the glycemic index of cane sugar, several vitamins and minerals, and has been named by the World Health Organization "the most sustainable sweetener in the world." Plus, the caramel-like flavor is undeniably delicious. It can be used as a 1:1 substitute for white or brown sugar.

## COCONUT WATER

A little sweet, a little salty, and incredibly refreshing, fresh coconut water is a true experience. Extracted from young Thai coconuts (sold in health food stores and Asian markets), this hydrating beverage is a natural electrolyte power-house, rich in the organic salts and minerals that are lost during exercise, sweating, or simply general dehydration. Coconut water has taken off commercially, and is now available pre-packaged in the juice and water sections of most markets. The packaged varieties are nowhere near as heavenly as a freshly cracked young coconut, but will still offer many of the same benefits, and have a longer shelf life, making them easy to keep on hand. Look for brands that are 100 percent pure with no added sugar.

Medjool dates are the among the most popular varieties.

## DATES

The extra-sweet fruit of the date palm has to be one of my favorite treats, period. Known as "nature's candy" by farmers and consumers alike, fresh dates are soft and smooth, and offer a caramel-like sweetness. Dates provide instant energy in the form of glucose and are one of the best natural sources of potassium (containing up to three times more potassium, ounce per ounce, than bananas). They are also full of dietary fiber, iron, vitamin A, magnesium, and many B vitamins as well. And a handful of dates equal a serving of fruit! With the highest natural sugar content of any fruit, I use dates frequently as a natural sweetener in my dessert recipes to replace the empty calories of refined sugar. There are many different types of dates, ranging in sweetness and softness; the most popular include the Medjool, Zahidi, and Honey varieties.

## EFA OILS

Oils high in essential fatty acids (EFAs) include hemp oil, flax oil, and various commercial blends (made from superfood seeds). The way I see it, if you're going to use an oil for non-cooking purposes, why not get the benefits of anti-inflammatory

EFAs and the beautiful flavor of healthy seeds at the same time? EFA oils offer that superfood-style boost. In my kitchen, I use an EFA oil formulation called Vega Antioxidant EFA Oil Blend. It's worth buying, as, in addition to hemp and flax oils, it includes a unique antioxidant-rich blend of pomegranate, green tea, cumin, blueberry, black raspberry, and cranberry seed oils. It tastes incredible, and I've yet to find an oil that trumps it in the nutrition department. When the recipes in this book call for "EFA oil," they will all work with hemp oil, flax oil, Vega Antioxidant EFA Oil Blend, or most other commercial EFA blends.

## FRUITS

Just because a fruit isn't a top "superfruit," that doesn't rule it out as great food choice. Every fruit has a unique portfolio of benefits, particularly in the vitamin department. Most fruits also contain some level of antioxidants and phytochemicals, just not in the same concentration as their more "super" cousins. Fruits help us manage our instinctual sweet tooth in the very best way possible, while adding fiber and extra nutrients. Unfortunately, fruits with edible skins often contain high concentrations of pesticide residues, so be sure to purchase organic whenever possible.

Some of the most health-giving fruits include figs, mangos, guavas, pineapples, cherries, prunes/plums, red grapes, lemons/limes, and grapefruit, as well as the ever-popular apples, oranges, and bananas. Fruits with edible skins are more important to buy organic than ones with an inedible peel (like bananas). Farmers' markets will have local, seasonal, and even sometimes heirloom breeds of your favorite fresh fruits to keep your diet fresh and full of exciting variety. I have found locally grown exotics like strawberry guavas and rose apples before, each of which were available for just a few weeks. Seeking out local fresh fruit quickly turns grocery shopping into a treasure hunt for treats.

## HERBS & SPICES

A good herb and spice collection is like having a well-stocked jewelry box: simply pick out a couple of accessories for an instant enhancement. While many conventional recipes rely upon large amounts of unhealthy fat, sugar, salt, and refined food for flavor, herbs and spices are the go-to healthy heroes that can provide sensational taste without the detrimental pricetag. Keeping an herb pot growing with a few favorite herbs is a great incentive to use them more often, but I also love having some key powders on hand as well. It never ceases to amaze me what these beautiful, clean, natural flavors can bring out in even the simplest whole foods.

Every herb and spice has its own unique set of medicinal properties, many of which are superfood-like in composition, but are limited in terms of edible quantity by their intense flavor. Leafy green herbs like parsley, basil, tarragon, and mint are wonderful superfoods that can be used in larger quantities. Other great spices to have on hand include bay leaves, paprika (the smoked variety is extra flavorful), chipotle powder, cayenne, cinnamon, and nutmeg. Though not true spices, I also always have a stash of garlic powder and onion powder—they can transform even a simple bowl of rice into something delectable. As always, check the packaging on spices to ensure they have nothing added, such as preservatives or salt.

## KOMBUCHA

Yes, it sounds strange: a fermented drink made out of a symbiotic culture of bacteria and yeast, then "brewed" in tea for a couple weeks. Yet regardless of its quirky origins, kombucha has been considered a premium health tonic for centuries. Like many fermented foods, kombucha contains an exceptional quantity of energizing enzymes, vitamins, and beneficial "friendly" bacteria. Many people report enhanced digestion, a slight energy boost, and an overall "good feeling" from drinking kombucha. It's a cheap, easy, and interesting project to make at home, but most health food stores now stock their shelves with this beverage due to increasing demands. Kombucha often comes in different flavors, which usually contain various teas and added fruit juice. The original flavor of kombucha can range from apple juice to champagne, usually with a slight vinegar undertone and a mild effervescence. Kombucha does contain a minute amount of alcohol, usually under 0.5 percent.

## LUCUMA POWDER

Lucuma powder is a finely milled powder made from freeze-dried lucuma fruit, which is native to South America. It provides a distinctively sweet flavor and full-bodied, maple-like taste, but is very low in sugars—making lucuma a welcome addition to smoothies and desserts. Plus, with naturally occurring beta-carotene, niacin, and iron,

Although just an unassuming green fruit on the outside, lucuma's sweet interior flesh is the color of a mango.

lucuma powder is a prime antidote to notorious "empty calorie" sweeteners. Lucuma powder may even be used as a partial gluten-free flour substitute in sweet baked goods. It may seem like an unnecessary specialty item, but lucuma's flavor is truly unmatched, and I consider it my "secret ingredient" in many smoothies and sweet recipes.

## MESQUITE POWDER

Native Americans often relied upon the ground-up sweet pods of the mesquite bush as a staple food, even using them as a bartering tool with neighboring tribes. Today, mesquite powder is of particular value to those looking to balance blood sugar levels since its sugars are derived from fructose (which does not require insulin to digest). Mesquite also contains lysine (an essential amino acid often deficient in plant-based diets), and notable quantities of protein, calcium, magnesium, potassium, iron, and zinc. Mesquite powder is a natural flavor match for cacao, and is excellent when used in desserts, smoothies, and even baking.

## MISO PASTE

Made from fermented soybeans, grains, or rice, miso acts as a full-bodied salty flavoring, containing a vast amount of enzymes, healthy minerals like zinc, and even elusive vitamins such as B-12. There are many varieties of miso, which vary in color and flavor potency. Yellow and white miso tend to be the lightest in flavor (and slightly sweet), brown miso is less sweet and a little saltier, and red miso is very potent and carries the strongest flavor.

**Note:** Unless otherwise specified, all recipes in this book are made using brown rice miso for a medium flavor, although other miso varieties may be easily substituted based on availability and flavor preference. If avoiding soy, look for rice or garbanzo miso. If using a soy-based miso, be sure to buy an organic variety—nearly all conventionally grown soy is a GMO crop, and thus, worth avoiding.

## NUTRITIONAL YEAST

A by-product of molasses, nutritional yeast has a salty, almost cheese-like taste that can be used as a flavor enhancer when sprinkled on top or mixed into foods. Sold in flakes or powder, nutritional yeast also contains B vitamins, minerals, protein, and has reportedly been used as an immune-enhancing supplement. Do not confuse nutritional yeast with brewer's yeast—the flavor is entirely different and the latter not particularly desirable.

## NUTS AND SEEDS

The embryo of all plants, nuts and seeds are extremely high in life-sustaining nutrients, including healthy fats, minerals, protein, and fiber. The line between a superfood seed and a "regular" seed need not be set in stone; and with the exception of peanuts (which are susceptible to a carcinogenic mold called aflatoxin), there isn't a culinary nut or seed that does not have genuine benefits. Among others, I always keep almonds, cashews, walnuts, sunflower seeds, sesame seeds, and pumpkin seeds around the kitchen in glass canning jars. These great foods are just waiting to be blended into a healthy "milk" (see page 224), ground into nut "meat," or used to lend a satisfying texture to recipes. They are a staple.

Additionally, cereal grains (like oats) and legumes (like beans or lentils) are also biologically considered seeds. They are indispensable in the kitchen, high in nutrition, inexpensive, and easy to store long-term. Store nuts and seeds in the refrigerator or freezer to make them last even longer.

## SEA SALT

You'll likely notice that sea salt is recommended in my recipes, as opposed to table salt. This is because the salty flavor of sea salt is more than just sodium. It is also a collection of trace minerals, including potassium, magnesium, calcium, and iodine. Additionally, sea salt has a subtly complex flavor that livens up recipes beautifully. There's nothing to be ashamed of in being a salt snob.

## SHOYU

"Shoyu" is actually the Japanese term for soy sauce, and usually is composed of soy, wheat, water, and salt. It offers a slightly sweeter flavor than Chinese soy sauce, and is excellent in marinades and Asian-influenced dishes. Nama Shoyu, which refers to an unpasteurized or "raw" form of this ingredient, may be used in its place. If neither are available (or if wheat must be avoided due to a gluten-free diet), regular soy sauce can also be used as a direct substitute for shoyu in any of the recipes in this book.

**Note:** Since shoyu is a soy product, it is especially important to buy organic, to avoid consuming conventionally grown GMO soybeans.

## STEVIA

Stevia is one of my favorite secret weapons in the kitchen. In fact, the only reason I can't call it a bona fide superfood is because it doesn't contain any real nutrition . . . but that's not to say it's without benefits.

Stevia is derived from a leaf—an all-natural herb that tastes profoundly sweet to the tongue, yet has no calories, carbohydrates, or sugars. It feels like cheating! Some people can taste a hint of bitterness in stevia, and it should be noted that the type of sweetness it adds is not a full-rounded

Natural stevia can be grown as a sweet garden herb.

sweetness like a traditional sugar. I categorize stevia as more of a flavor extender: an herb that will stretch small amounts of other sweeteners, allowing less sugar overall to be used in a recipe. What a deal! Since every stevia company on the market has a product with a different sweetness potency, it is very difficult to dictate specific quantities to use. (See the Ingredient Resources Guide on page 228 in the back of this book for brand recommendations.) Therefore, I suggest looking at stevia like a sweet version of salt: use to taste. Though the milled green (whole leaf) stevia is great for tea, the white refined stevia (and liquid stevia extracts) are much more sweet and infinitely more versatile. A tip for new stevia users: begin by using just a fraction of what you think you might need. Stevia is profoundly potent and even a speck will make a flavor difference! Many people who "don't like stevia" because they find it "bitter" discover that they simply used too much when first trying it. Stevia's sweet benefits make it an ingredient definitely worth trying to master.

## TAHINI

In many cultures around the world, tahini—also known as sesame butter or paste—is a staple food product. It's just like a smooth almond or peanut butter, except it's made from calcium-rich sesame seeds instead. Tahini provides an earthy richness to recipes that is unmatched by any other ingredient. Due to increasing popularity, this condiment is becoming more available, branching out from health food stores, and now included in many conventional grocery markets as well. It's generally made from roasted sesame seeds, which offer a full flavor, but raw varieties can sometimes be sourced

as well (although they are significantly more costly). Either roasted or raw tahini can be used for the recipes in this book.

## UMEBOSHI (UME) PLUM VINEGAR

Briny with a unique tang, think of this special condiment as half vinegar and half a salty agent. Umeboshi plums are a Japanese specialty: pickled unripe plums that have been soaked with shiso (beefsteak) leaves and sea salt. Once the plums are removed (which can be used in cooking as well), the leftover brine is naturally fermented and a beautiful light pink vinegar full of healthy organic acids forms. Umeboshi plum vinegar gives recipes such a gorgeous complexity that it's become a staple in my pantry; luckily, it's becoming a staple at health food stores, too.

## VEGETABLES

It may seem obvious, but eating (land-grown) vegetables is an absolute essential part of being in tip-top superfoodified shape. If superfoods are the "butter," then vegetables are the "bread." Vegetables primarily provide minerals, some vitamins, amino acids and protein, fiber, and varying levels of antioxidants and phytochemicals. Of course, it is best to consume vegetables that score the highest on the ANDI charts, but in general, there are only three real veggie rules: eat a wide variety, eat as organic as possible, and eat as many as possible. Regardless of micronutrient content ranking, I never, ever feel guilty about eating vegetables—they always have something to offer.

much more. A dehydrator can even turn a single ingredient, like a banana, into the most delectable natural candy: a sweet and taffy-like banana chew. But creativity aside, the second advantage of dehydrating is an excitingly healthy one. Cooking at lower temperatures allows a greater quantity of nutrients (like healthy enzymes and naturally-occurring vitamins) to be preserved—a contrast to the inevitable nutrient loss that occurs when these sensitive ingredients are exposed to high heat processes.

Admittedly, dehydrators are not without their flaws. Perhaps the most blatant offense of this appliance is the sweet, sweet time it takes in cooking food. Depending on the type of recipe and the temperature used, some food requires sitting as long as twelve hours inside the dehydrator box before being ready. And trust me: with all kinds of delicious smells wafting out, the wait can be a difficult one. This is not a preferred method for those short on patience.

Dehydrated foods are also much more sensitive to moisture than cooked foods, so a humid environment not only affects the cooking time, but can also turn fresh and crispy crackers disappointingly soft within the span of a day. This problem is easily avoided by storing dehydrated food in a tight-seal, moisture-proof container.

Dehydrators are the least necessary of the appliances listed here; there are weeks at a time in my house where the dehydrator will sit quietly unused. Nonetheless, this appliance is a snack-making machine, capable of producing exceptionally delicious and healthy treats that often cannot otherwise be made at home. A dehydrator is not required for any of the recipes in this book, but can be used to boost the nutritional content of a few.

## ECO PAN: THE CLEANER, GREENER WAY TO FRY

At one time, nonstick frying pans were the most exciting thing to happen to the stove top. Their useful cooking surface did more than just free up some time away from the steel-wool scrubber; these pans also enabled healthier cooking, as their nonstick surface allowed using substantially less oil to prevent foods from sticking. A great idea. Unfortunately, we've now come to find out this technology comes at a price: the nonstick materials used in these pans (the most notorious being Teflon, but true of most nonstick pans in general) contain extremely toxic chemicals. These chemicals, which include the known carcinogen PTFE, break down and are released as the pan gets hotter . . . leaching into the food while cooking. It goes without saying: these pans are not safe to use, unquestionably negate any benefits of healthier cooking, and should be avoided entirely.

Since the truth about this nonstick cookware became public knowledge, the switch back to "normal" aluminum or cast iron pans was inevitable, and more oil has seeped back into our cooked fare again. Luckily, a new wave of smart cookware has arrived on the scene: "eco pans." These new "green" pans utilize eco-friendly materials, such as ceramic, to produce a nonstick surface that is not only ideal for healthier, easier cooking, but is nontoxic and recognized as safe to use. Some of these pans are even constructed out of recycled materials.

Whenever a "nonstick pan" is mentioned in the recipes in this book (or any book for that matter), promise me you'll use an eco pan. There are many good brands available that will support your efforts to live a green, nontoxic, and healthy lifestyle!

# PART THREE

# RECIPES

This symbol ✖ represents a superfood.

# BREAKFASTS

*You know it's going to be a good day when you're superfood-fueled first thing in the morning. Nutrient-dense breakfasts are more than a mere commercial catchphrase stuck on cereal boxes—they set the tone for energy levels throughout the day. I would even go so far as to say that if you're going to make just one meal each day a superfood meal, breakfast should have the honor. You'll find it's a perfect time to load up on sweet berries, satisfying super seeds, and maybe even sneak in a sprinkle of powdered superfood goodness like maca or acai.*

# BANANA SEED BREAD

*This recipe fills the whole house with the alluring scent of fresh-baked banana goodness, resulting in an ultra-moist, sweet treat. Secret ingredients—including flax and hemp—add extra fiber, protein, and EFAs that everybody can appreciate. Plus, use of low-glycemic sweeteners like coconut sugar, agave, and lucuma help to make this a superior version of traditional recipes as well. Be warned: It's even more delicious the next day!*

3 tablespoons flaxseed powder

⅓ cup almond milk, unsweetened

1½ cups whole wheat flour*

¼ cup lucuma powder

1 tablespoon mesquite powder

1 teaspoon baking soda

1 tablespoon baking powder

¾ teaspoon sea salt

¼ cup melted coconut oil, plus extra for baking pan

⅔ cup + 1 tablespoon coconut sugar

2 tablespoons agave nectar

½ teaspoon coconut extract (optional)

1½ cup mashed very ripe bananas (about 3–4 bananas)

½ cup hemp seeds

*If following a gluten-free diet, use gluten-free flour, available through natural food stores or online (see ingredient resources on page 228).

Preheat oven to 350° F. Lightly grease a 9 x 5 x 3-inch loaf pan with coconut oil.

Mix the flaxseed powder with almond milk in a small cup. Set aside for 5–10 minutes to let the ingredients "gel."

In a medium-sized bowl, mix together the flour, lucuma powder, mesquite powder, baking soda, baking powder, and salt. In a large bowl, blend the coconut oil, ⅔ cup coconut sugar, prepared flax mixture, agave nectar, coconut extract, and mashed bananas until well combined. Mix the dry ingredients in with the wet ingredients until combined. Fold in the hemp seeds.

Transfer mixture to the prepared loaf pan. Sprinkle the remaining tablespoon of coconut sugar over the top of the batter. Bake for 45–50 minutes, or until the top is browned and a toothpick comes out clean when inserted into the bread. Flip onto a baking rack and let cool before serving. After completely cooled, wrap in plastic wrap for storage; will keep for up to one week.

**Serving Suggestion:** Enjoy with a smear of Buttery Spread (page 160) and Acai Berry Jam (page 70).

## USING FLAX AND CHIA AS "EGGS" IN BAKING

Flaxseed powder and chia seed powder are tremendously helpful baking tools. Due to their naturally high amount of mucilage, each has the ability to quickly form a gel-like substance when soaked in liquid, similar in consistency to a raw egg. While this "gel" will not rise like a cooked egg, it does serve as an excellent binder in baked recipes. As long as the recipe contains other agents to help it rise (such as baking soda, gluten, etc.), this beneficial superseed formula can be used in place of raw eggs with great success.

### FOR THE EQUIVALENT OF TWO EGGS:

Mix 2 tablespoons ground flaxseed or chia seed powder with ⅓ cup water or nut milk (see page 224). Stir. Wait 5–10 minutes, and stir one more time. Ready to use.

# BIG BERRY MUFFINS

## MAKES 12 MUFFINS

*These low-fat muffins go all out on packing in as many fresh berries as possible. Using an assortment of berries—like blackberries, raspberries, blueberries, and chopped strawberries—offers more than just a wide range of nutrients, they're also extra fun to eat . . . kind of like a treasure hunt full of delicious fruity surprises.*

1 ¾ cups whole wheat flour*

2 teaspoons baking powder

½ teaspoon baking soda

½ teaspoon sea salt

½ cup cashew milk (page 224), or store-bought nut milk of choice

½ cup applesauce

⅓ cup maple syrup

2 tablespoons melted coconut oil

1 teaspoon fresh lemon zest

1 ½ cups mixed fresh berries (such as blueberries, blackberries, raspberries, etc.)

1 tablespoon coconut sugar

*If following a gluten-free diet, use gluten-free flour, available through natural food stores or online (see Ingredient Resources Guide on page 228).

Preheat the oven to 350° F. Line a 12-cup muffin tin with paper liners, or lightly grease each cup with coconut oil.

Stir together the flour, baking powder, baking soda, and salt in a large bowl. In a smaller bowl, whisk the nut milk, applesauce, maple syrup, coconut oil, and lemon zest together. Add the wet ingredients into the dry, and mix together until just combined. The batter will be lumpy, but resist over-mixing, as it will cause the muffins to be dense. Gently fold in the berries, then spoon the batter equally into the 12 prepared muffin cups. Sprinkle each muffin top with a dusting of coconut sugar. Bake the muffins for about 25–30 minutes, or until the tops begin to turn golden brown and a toothpick comes out clean when inserted into a muffin. Let cool for a few minutes before serving.

# GOLDENBERRY PANCAKES

## MAKES 8 MEDIUM PANCAKES

*"Goldenberry" sounds like the kind of fruit you want to wake up to. Here, this sweet and tart fruit is complemented by bright orange flavors to make a light and fluffy extra special pancake. Plus, using a smart ingredient set like this one (be gone, white flour!) turns empty calories into calories with benefits. When pancakes call, try these flavorful good guys.*

1 cup whole wheat flour*

½ teaspoon baking soda

2 teaspoons baking powder

pinch sea salt

1 cup fresh orange juice

½ teaspoon fresh orange zest

1 teaspoon vanilla extract

1 tablespoon maple syrup

2 tablespoons melted coconut oil, plus a little extra for cooking

⅓ cup dried goldenberries, chopped

maple syrup, for serving

Buttery Spread (page 160), for serving (optional)

*If following a gluten-free diet, use gluten-free flour, available through natural food stores or online (see ingredient resources on page 228).

In a medium bowl, mix together the flour, baking soda, baking powder, and sea salt. In a blender, mix the orange juice, orange zest, vanilla, maple syrup, and 2 tablespoons of coconut oil into a smooth liquid. (Using a blender will ensure the coconut oil homogenizes with the liquid, to produce a fluffier pancake.) Add the dry ingredients into the blender, and blend again for just a moment until combined (do not overmix). Fold in the goldenberries by hand.

Warm a skillet over medium heat, and brush lightly with coconut oil. For each pancake, drop about ¼ cup of batter into the pan, smoothing it out slightly with the back of a spoon to flatten. Cook until bubbles form and begin to burst on the top, then flip and cook until golden brown and cooked through. To serve, top with maple syrup and Buttery Spread, if desired.

### SUPERFOOD TIP
Many baking powders contain aluminum, which can be potentially toxic. Choose a brand that specifically states "aluminum-free" and avoid the risk.

# LEMON-COCONUT BREAKFAST BARS

## MAKES 16 2 X 2-INCH SQUARES

*Good-choice breakfast bars have a combination of simple sugars for instant energy, complex carbohydrates for more lasting energy, and a bit of healthy fat to further smooth over the morning hungries. These sweet lemony treats are the perfect canvas for a beautiful collection of natural ingredients like chia seeds, dates, oats, and coconut.*

1½ tablespoons chia seeds

3 tablespoons fresh lemon juice

1 cup oat flour*

½ teaspoon baking powder

pinch of sea salt

¾ cup + 2 tablespoons shredded dried coconut, divided

2 tablespoons fresh lemon zest

2 tablespoons coconut oil, melted

2 tablespoons applesauce

¼ cup maple syrup or agave nectar

½ cup soft Medjool dates (about 5 or 6), pits removed

*If following a gluten-free diet, use gluten-free flour, available through natural food stores or online (see ingredient resources on page 228).

Preheat the oven to 300° F. Lightly grease an 8 × 8-inch baking pan.

In a small bowl, mix the chia seeds and lemon juice together. Set aside for 20 minutes to allow the chia seeds to become saturated and bulk up, stirring once halfway through.

Meanwhile, in a medium bowl, mix together the oat flour, baking powder, salt, and ¾ cup coconut flakes. Sprinkle in the lemon zest and mix again until distributed. In a separate bowl, combine the coconut oil, applesauce, and maple syrup or agave nectar. Mix in the soaked chia seeds. Chop the pitted Medjool dates very finely, and mix in with the other wet ingredients. Pour the wet ingredients into the dry, and stir until blended. Spread the mixture into the prepared baking pan, using a spatula to flatten out the surface. Sprinkle the remaining 2 tablespoons of coconut on top, patting it down lightly into the mixture.

Bake for 25–28 minutes, until the edges begin to turn golden brown. While warm, cut into 12–16 squares.

# CHOCOLATE ENERGY BAR

### MAKES 8 BARS

*The best in grab-and-go ( . . . and go . . . and yeah, still going . . . ) snacks. The convenient nutrition of these yummy bars has made them a staple in my kitchen—I double the batch, wrap them up, and stick them in the freezer until I need a "something" when I'm on the go. Plus, these are a wonderful excuse to enjoy chocolate at any time of the day (yes, even for breakfast).*

1½ cups soft Medjool dates (about 15 or 16), pits removed

¼ cup raw almonds

¼ cup raw cashews

¼ cup cacao powder

3 tablespoons cacao nibs

6 tablespoons hemp seeds

1 tablespoon chia seeds

2 teaspoons maca powder

1 teaspoon mesquite powder (optional—enhances flavor)

2 tablespoons raw nuts/seeds (use favorite kind)

¼ cup dried fruit (use favorite kind)

### SUPERFOOD TIP

Mix it up by using different kinds of nuts and seeds (like sacha inchi seeds or macadamia nuts), and different dried fruits (like goji berries, dried cherries, or dried blueberries).

Grind all ingredients together in a food processor except for the last 2 tablespoons of nuts/seeds and ¼ cup of dried fruit, until a coarse dough has formed (this process may take a couple of minutes). Stop the machine and check the consistency: pinch the dough between two fingers and make sure it sticks together easily so that your bars don't end up crumbly. If the dough is too dry, add a tiny amount of water—about ½ teaspoon at a time—and blend again until the desired stickiness is achieved. Add the last 2 tablespoons of nuts/seeds and dried fruit and pulse several times until just coarsely chopped to give the bars a nice texture.

Place a large sheet of plastic wrap on a flat surface and spill out the dough on top. Gather into a solid mass in the center; then use the sides of the plastic to wrap over the dough as tightly as possible, pressing, pounding, and shaping into a compact 1-inch thick rectangle.

When solid, remove the wrap and cut into 8 bars. (For extra clean cuts, you can place the bar in the freezer for 30 minutes before cutting.) Wrap and keep in the freezer for long-term storage.

**Variation:** Add hemp protein, a teaspoon of freeze-dried wheatgrass powder, or a bit of chlorella to boost the protein and nutrition even further.

# THE ULTIMATE ENERGY BAR

## MAKES 8–10 BARS

*Energy bars, like smoothies, are a perfect opportunity to recharge with the condensed nutrition of superfoods. Literally packed with superfruits, quality nuts, and special seeds, this bar is an enviably amazing on-the-go breakfast or snack.*

- 1 cup dried mulberries
- ½ cup dried goji berries
- ½ cup dried goldenberries
- 2 tablespoons raw cacao nibs
- ½ cup raw cashews
- 1 cup chopped raw walnuts
- 1 cup soft Medjool dates (about 10 or 11), pits removed
- ½ cup chopped roasted sacha inchi seeds (optional)

### SUPERFOOD TIP
Wrap bars up in plastic wrap (individually for grab-and-go snacks or together for eco-friendly storage) and keep in the freezer for long-term use.

In a food processer, grind all ingredients except the sacha inchi together until a coarse dough has formed (this process may take a couple of minutes). Stop the machine and check the consistency: pinch the dough between two fingers and make sure it sticks together easily so that your bars don't end up crumbly. If the dough is too dry, add a tiny amount of water—about ½ teaspoon at a time—and blend again until the desired stickiness is achieved.

Place a large sheet of plastic wrap on a flat surface and spill out the dough on top. Gather into a solid mass in the center, and sprinkle the sacha inchi on top. Stretch the sides of the plastic to wrap over the dough as tightly as possible, pressing, pounding, and shaping into a compact 1-inch thick rectangle. Once you've formed what looks like one very large energy bar, remove the wrap and cut into 8–10 individual bars.

# HOT QUINOA BOWL

*Rolled quinoa flakes are a high-protein, gluten-free, mineral-rich (and utterly crave-worthy) answer to oatmeal. Warm up with this extra-fast recipe, and get creative with your favorite superfood toppings, like chopped or dried yacon slices, dried goji berries, dried mulberries, or coconut sugar with cinnamon. Even just plain, this recipe earns a spot among my favorite breakfasts.*

1 cup unsweetened almond milk or hemp milk (page 224)

⅓ cup quinoa flakes

dash of sea salt

superfood toppings of choice

In a medium saucepan, bring the almond or hemp milk to a boil. Add the quinoa flakes and salt; mix together, and turn off the heat. Let rest for 3 minutes to allow the quinoa flakes to cook through, then serve with desired toppings.

# PROTEIN QUINOA BOWL

MAKES 1 SERVING

*This is a mixture I like to make on days where I need a little extra "oomph." Because the hemp protein has chlorophyll in it, the mixture will display a less-than-lovely shade of green, and I'm not going to lie—it's pretty much the ugly duckling of the breakfast bowl world. Nonetheless, the yummy flavor and mega-nutrition are convincing enough—this recipe provides sustainable energy for hours.*

1 batch Hot Quinoa Bowl (above)

1 tablespoon hemp protein powder (or more if you're into it)

1 teaspoon maca powder

½ tablespoon almond butter

½ banana, sliced

maple syrup, for drizzling

Make the Hot Quinoa Bowl as directed above. When warm and ready, mix in the hemp protein powder, maca powder, almond butter, and banana slices. Stir well. Drizzle with a little maple syrup just before serving, if desired.

# BANANA-HEMP GRANOLA

## MAKES ABOUT 8 CUPS

*Take advantage of flavor-friends banana and hemp seed with this exceptional granola recipe.
I seriously can't stop eating this when there's a fresh batch around . . . and when you check
out the ingredients, you'll see why I'm more than okay with that.*

¾ cup mashed very ripe bananas
(about 2 bananas)

⅔ cup soft Medjool dates, (about
6 or 7), pits removed

1 tablespoon vanilla extract

¼ teaspoon sea salt

¼ cup smooth almond butter

3 cups oats*

 ½ cup hemp seeds

*For gluten-free granola, use gluten-
free oats, available through natural
food stores or online (see Ingredient
Resources Guide on page 228).

Preheat the oven to 300° F. Line a cookie sheet with parchment paper
and set aside.

Place the mashed bananas, dates, vanilla extract, and sea salt into
a single-serving blender or food processor. Puree until as smooth
as possible, getting the dates to blend with the bananas. Stop the
machine, add the almond butter, and blend again briefly.

In a large bowl, toss together the oats and the hemp seeds. Pour the
banana blend on top, and mix until the oats are well coated. Spread
the mixture out evenly across the prepared cookie sheet and bake in
the oven, setting a timer for 30 minutes. After half an hour, take
the granola out of the oven and use a spatula to flip and mix the
granola, breaking up the large clumps to ensure even baking. Return
to the oven and continue baking for another 20–30 minutes, until
the granola begins to turn golden brown. (Total baking time is 50–60
minutes.) Remove from the oven and let cool to room temperature
on the hot baking sheet before transferring to a storage container.

**Serving suggestion:** Serve with almond milk, fresh bananas or strawberries, and raw cacao nibs.

# CINNAMON-ALMOND GRANOLA WITH MULBERRIES

## MAKES ABOUT 6 CUPS

*Though the heavenly smell of this granola while it's baking is almost reason enough to make it, just wait until you take a taste. Full of crunchy, groovy flavor that's way lower in fat than most other granolas, this mix is the perfect breakfast, snack, or parfait topping. I like to bake a double batch and keep this beneficial mix in a big jar on the counter, grabbing swipes throughout the day. Baking it at a low temperature does more than prevent the granola from burning, it also protects the healthy EFA fats in the flax and chia.*

3 cups old fashioned rolled oats*

½ cup raw almonds, hand-chopped into small chunks

3 tablespoons flaxseed powder

3 tablespoons chia seeds

1 teaspoon cinnamon powder

¼ teaspoon sea salt

1 cup applesauce

⅓ cup coconut sugar

1 tablespoon vanilla extract

1 teaspoon almond extract (optional)

½ tablespoon melted coconut oil

1 cup dried mulberries

*For gluten-free granola, use gluten-free oats, available through natural food stores or online (see Ingredient Resources Guide on page 228).

Preheat the oven to 300° F. Line a cookie sheet with parchment paper and set aside.

In a large bowl, combine the oats, almonds, flax, chia, cinnamon, and sea salt and mix well. In a separate small bowl, mix together the applesauce, coconut sugar, vanilla extract, almond extract (if using), and coconut oil. Pour the liquid mixture into the oats bowl, and toss until combined.

Spread the granola evenly across the prepared cookie sheet and bake in the oven, setting a timer for 30 minutes. After half an hour, take the granola out of the oven and use a spatula to flip and mix the granola, using the edge to break up the large clumps to ensure even baking. Return to the oven and continue baking until the granola begins to turn golden brown, about another 20–30 minutes (50–60 minutes total baking time). Remove from oven and immediately mix in mulberries. Let cool completely on the baking pan, then store in an airtight container.

# SPICED CHIA PORRIDGE

## MAKES 2–4 SERVINGS

*As the Mayan word for "strength," chia has long been documented as providing a profoundly sustainable form of energy. It comes as no surprise, then, that this satisfying breakfast recipe is ideal for energy-rich morning fuel . . . giving regular old oatmeal a run for the money. When soaked in liquid, the chia seeds bulk up into a thick porridge that's easy to make in the evening, leaving breakfast ready to rock by the morning. You can also try one of the faster variations for a more instant form of chia gratification.*

2½ cups water

⅔ cup soft Medjool dates (about 6 or 7), pits removed

¼ cup raw cashews

¼ cup hemp seeds

½ teaspoon pumpkin pie spice, or cinnamon powder

⅓ cup chia seeds

¼ cup dried mulberries

3 tablespoons dried goji berries

fresh fruit, for serving

### SUPERFOOD TIP

For an extra energy boost, use brewed yerba mate or green tea instead of water when making the sweet "milk" blend.

Combine the water, dates, cashews, hemp seeds, and pumpkin pie spice in a blender and process to form a smooth "milk." Pour into a large bowl and stir in the chia seeds. Let sit for ten minutes to allow the chia seeds to plump up, then stir again and let rest for 10 additional minutes. Mix in the mulberries and goji berries. Cover and place in the refrigerator overnight to allow the flavors to develop and the dried berries to plump up. In the morning, transfer a few scoops of the porridge to a serving bowl, and top with fresh fruit like chopped bananas or berries. Will keep for several days, refrigerated.

**Lazier, faster variation:** Use 1½ cups of store-bought unsweetened almond milk in place of the water, medjool dates, cashews, and hemp seeds. In a medium bowl, combine the milk with the pumpkin pie spice and a desired sweetener to taste (such as stevia, coconut sugar, agave nectar, or maple syrup). Stir in the chia seeds. Let sit for 10 minutes to allow the chia seeds to plump up, then stir again and let rest for an additional 10 minutes. Stir once more. Add a few scoops to a serving bowl, and mix in dried mulberries, goji berries, and fresh fruit (if desired).

**Hot, instant variation:** Mix the milk, spice, and sweetener (using either of the methods above) in a saucepan over medium heat. Add the chia seeds, plus 2 tablespoons of hemp seeds and ½ cup rolled oats, and stir well. Bring to a simmer and cook for 2 minutes, then add in dried berries and remove from heat. Let sit for 2–3 minutes to allow the oats and chia seeds to swell. Add fresh fruit if desired.

# MANGO & BERRY PARFAIT

*When whipped up, this mango puree reminds me of a lightly fruity yogurt. It's smooth and sexy and super-fast to make. You can enjoy this parfait as part of a leisurely weekend brunch, or put it in a container and take it to the office for a healthy snack.*

⅔ cup water

⅔ cup raw cashews

¼ cup fresh lime juice

2 teaspoons agave nectar, or a dash of stevia

2½ cups chopped mango (about 2 mangos), peel and pit discarded

2 cups raspberries, blackberries, blueberries, or strawberries

Blend the water, cashews, lime juice, and agave (or stevia) into a very smooth cream. Add in the chopped mango and blend again into a whip. Place a large dollop into a serving bowl and top generously with fresh berries.

**Variation:** Mix in 2 tablespoons acai or maqui powder for a delicious antioxidant boost. Granola makes an excellent topping as well.

## SUPERFOOD TIP

If the cashews and water are not blending smoothly enough, let the mixture rest for an hour, then blend again. This will allow the cashew pieces to become saturated with water, softening their texture and making them easier to cream.

# ACAI BOWL

MAKES ONE SERVING

*After my friend took a trip to Brazil and came back raving about the acai bowls he enjoyed every morning, I knew my breakfast needed an upgrade. This simple rendition of Brazilian superfood fare is a truly feel-good way to start the day. Think of it like a thick, antioxidant-rich smoothie you can eat with a spoon.*

1 frozen banana (see below)
2 tablespoons acai powder
¼ cup unsweetened almond milk
dash of stevia, to taste (or
    1 tablespoon maple syrup)
granola (page 62 or 63), optional
fresh fruit, optional

Blend the frozen banana, acai powder, almond milk, and a bit of sweetener into a thick, smooth consistency. Spoon out into a bowl and top with granola and fresh fruit, if desired, or just enjoy plain.

## FROZEN BANANA 101

Frozen bananas are a superfood kitchen staple, serving two purposes. First, they provide a frosty ice cream-like texture to blended mixtures that's different from a fresh banana (meet your smoothie's new best friend). And second, frozen bananas are an excellent way to save bananas that are past their prime. Here are five steps to becoming a frozen banana pro:

ONE: For best results, use the ripest bananas possible. Brown is good!
TWO: Always peel the bananas prior to freezing them.
THREE: Slice the bananas into rounds before freezing; your blender's blades will thank you.
FOUR: Store in a large zip-lock bag, spreading out the slices into a flat layer so snapping
    off a frozen section is easy (no flat layer = frozen banana brick).
FIVE: As a general guide, one big handful of frozen banana slices is about one banana.

# ACAI BERRY JAM

MAKES ABOUT 1 CUP

*This jam is dense with nutrition, low in sugar, full of whole superfoods, and completely unprocessed. Featuring two all-star superfoods—acai and chia—it's a fantastic way to sneak extra antioxidants, essential fatty acids, and vital micronutrients into any diet. Acai's soft berry flavor results in a mild-tasting jam, which is as versatile as it is delicious. For a stronger taste, mix in ¼ cup muddled fresh berries (like raspberries or blackberries) before serving. Use on bread, with muffins, on top of desserts, or enjoy a solo spoonful with zero guilt!*

- 2½ tablespoons chia seeds
- ½ cup apple juice (fresh is best)
- 2 tablespoons acai powder
- 2 tablespoons maple syrup
- 1 tablespoon lemon juice
- ¼ cup muddled fresh berries, raspberries, etc., (optional)

Stir the chia seeds and apple juice together in a small bowl or glass. Let the mixture sit for 20–30 minutes, stirring once about halfway through. After the chia has formed a gel, mix in the acai powder, maple syrup, lemon juice, and optional fresh berries. For best results, allow the jam to sit for 30 minutes before serving, letting the flavors fully marry. This jam will last for about 1 week when kept in a sealed container and refrigerated.

**Variation:** For Maqui Berry Jam, substitute maqui powder for the acai.

> **SUPERFOOD TIP**
> Make this jam thicker or thinner to preference by slightly increasing or decreasing the amount of chia seeds used.

# GOLDENBERRY JAM

*Goldenberries naturally have a flavor that is reminiscent of marmalade, which is exactly what this jam reminds me of. It's free of added sugar, easy to make, and keeps in the refrigerator for about two weeks in a sealed container (although it's so good I've never been able to make it last that long).*

2 cups white grape juice

4 teaspoons agar agar flakes

1 cup dried goldenberries, finely chopped

a touch of stevia (optional)

---

### SUPERFOOD TIP

Jello cravings? Try agar agar. Traditionally used in Japanese cuisine, agar is a vegetarian gelling agent derived from a marine algae, and produces a gelatin-like substance when cooked with water. It has no color, imparts no taste, and easily adopts whatever flavors it is cooked with. Agar also has the unique ability to be re-melted and re-gelled many times without losing its strength.

---

In a small saucepan over medium heat, mix together the grape juice and the agar agar and bring to a simmer; stir constantly to prevent the flakes from sticking to the bottom and sides of the pan. Cook for about 5 minutes, or until the agar agar has completely dissolved and the juice is slightly reduced. Stir in the goldenberries and remove from heat. Mix in a touch of stevia to taste, if desired, to create a sweeter jam, and cover the pot. Let rest at room temperature for 30 minutes to allow the goldenberries to plump up.

Uncover and transfer to a small (single-serving) blender. Pulse a couple of times into a chunky mixture. (Alternatively, simply bruise the berries with the back of a spoon to release the seeds.) Transfer to a glass jar with a lid and refrigerate. After 1 hour, give the jam a stir to evenly distribute the goldenberries that may have sunk to the bottom with the rest of the jam (which will have begun to thicken). Return to the refrigerator to allow the jam to gel completely (about 2–3 hours).

Will keep for several weeks, refrigerated.

# SOUPS

*There's something very nurturing about soups, which are often viewed as the epitome of rejuvenation. Soups are also the perfect canvas for some of the most mineral-rich foods nature has to offer, including detoxifying sea vegetables, alkalizing greens, beautifying seeds, and comforting quinoa. You don't have to wait for a cold day either—there are several tantalizing raw soup options that pack in the antioxidants and vitamins.*

# ROASTED PUMPKIN SOUP

*Super-roots maca and yacon work together beautifully with pumpkin's richness, offering a flavorful way to recharge and energize. "Sugar Pie" pumpkins are tradionally used for pumpkin pies, as this small and sweet pumpkin variety yields a much more flavorful result than larger "conventional" pumpkins. (If pumpkins aren't in season, try the variation below.) Of course, to save time, you can use organic canned pumpkin, but fresh is always best.*

1 tablespoon coconut oil

1 cup sweet yellow onion, diced (about ½ medium onion)

2 large cloves garlic, minced

3 cups roasted sugar pie pumpkin, chopped into 1-inch chunks

1½ teaspoons smoked paprika (or regular paprika)

½ teaspoon sea salt

2 cups light coconut milk

⅓ cup pineapple juice

1 tablespoon yacon syrup, plus extra for serving

1 tablespoon maca powder

freshly cracked black pepper, to taste

Warm the coconut oil in a large pot over medium heat. Add the onions and garlic and cook for 4–5 minutes, or until onions begin to turn translucent. Add the pumpkin, paprika, and sea salt, and cook for a couple of minutes longer, stirring constantly. Pour in the coconut milk, pineapple juice, and 1 tablespoon yacon syrup. Bring the mixture to a boil, then reduce heat to a simmer. Cover, and cook for 15 minutes, or until vegetables are soft.

Transfer to a blender and add the maca powder. Puree the soup until smooth, then taste and adjust seasonings if desired. To serve, ladle soup into a serving bowl, drizzle with yacon syrup, and top with generously with freshly cracked black pepper.

**Variation:** Use roasted butternut squash in place of the pumpkin.

### SUPERFOOD TIP
Think carrots are the only way to good eyesight? Try pumpkin! These winter squashes contain a unique array of antioxidants that help scavenge free radicals in the lens of the eye and protect our vision.

## HOW TO ROAST A PUMPKIN

Preheat the oven to 375° F.

Cut the pumpkin in half and remove the seeds and stringy matter. Place the pumpkin, flesh-side up, on a baking sheet lined with parchment paper, and season with a few pinches of sea salt and black pepper. Rub ½ tablespoon of coconut oil on each pumpkin half, then flip the halves over to sit flesh-side down on the pan. Place in the oven and roast until the skin begins to brown and the flesh is tender—about 45–50 minutes.

Remove from the oven and let cool. When cool enough to handle, use a spoon to scoop out the flesh for use and discard the skin.

# KALE & BLACK-EYED PEA STEW

## MAKES 6–8 SERVINGS

*There's always something exciting about a pot of good stuff bubbling away on the stove. Especially when that "good stuff" includes powerful ingredients providing a balanced array of minerals, protein, and fiber. Adding the kale at the very end of the cooking ensures that it's softened enough to be enjoyed, without destroying all of its nutrition through heat. This is the kind of stew that eats like a meal.*

1 tablespoon coconut oil

2 cups white onions, diced (about 1 medium onion)

6 cloves garlic, minced

3 stalks celery, diced

1 red bell pepper, diced

1 tablespoon fresh oregano leaves, chopped

½ tablespoon fresh thyme leaves, chopped

¼ teaspoon chipotle powder

1 tablespoon smoked paprika

3 cups vegetable broth

3 cups water

2 tablespoons wakame flakes, ground/crushed into fine pieces

3 cups cooked black-eyed peas

1 head kale, stems discarded and leaves chopped

½ lemon, juiced

fresh parsley, chopped, for garnish

sea salt to taste

In a large pot, melt the coconut oil over medium heat. Add the onions and garlic and cook for 2 minutes, stirring occasionally. Add the celery and bell pepper and cook for a few minutes longer. Stir in the herbs and spices, cooking for about 30 seconds. Add the vegetable broth, water, wakame flakes, black-eyed peas, and a pinch of sea salt. Bring to a gentle simmer, and cook uncovered for 30 minutes, adding more water if needed. Taste, and adjust salt if desired. After the soup is fully cooked through, stir in the kale and keep over the heat for a minute longer—just enough to wilt the kale. Add the lemon juice and turn off the heat. Top with parsley and serve.

**Variation:** Add 1 cup diced smoked tofu when you add the black-eyed peas.

### SUPERFOOD TIP

Using smoked ingredients like chipotle powder and smoked paprika add an impressive depth of flavor to recipes without compromising nutrition through overcooking. Find these spices in most supermarkets, or from a retailer listed in the Ingredient Resources Guide (page 228).

# YELLOW PEA & SACHA INCHI CHOWDER

*The sacha inchi seeds really shine in this soup—they remain crisp during the cooking process, but take on an almost meaty flavor role as the ingredients marry while cooking. Meanwhile, favorite soup-superfood wakame melts away into the background, leaving only its high mineral content and a subtle savory flavor.*

1 tablespoon coconut oil

1 cup white onion, diced (about ½ medium onion)

1 stalk celery, diced

1 carrot, diced

1½ cups chopped tomato, pureed

2 tablespoons wakame flakes, ground/crushed into fine pieces

1 bay leaf

¾ cup dried yellow split peas

¼ cup chopped fresh parsley

1 quart vegetable stock

½ cup sacha inchi, finely chopped

water, for cooking

sea salt and freshly cracked black pepper, to taste

In a large pot, heat the coconut oil over medium heat. Add the onion, celery, carrot, as well as a pinch of salt, then sauté the vegetables until the onion is soft—about 7–8 minutes. Mix in the fresh tomato puree and cook for a minute or two longer. Add all of the remaining ingredients except salt and pepper, plus 1 cup of water. Cover, bring the mixture to a boil, then reduce to a simmer and cook for about 75 minutes, or until peas are soft. Add additional water to the pot if needed during the cooking process. Finally, adjust the salt if desired, and garnish with black pepper before serving.

# CHILLED CREAMY BEET SOUP

*A velvety-smooth texture and absolutely stunning fuchsia color make this simple soup a supremely impressive first course or light lunch. The beets can be roasted ahead of time for a faster turnaround; I always make more than the recipe calls for and use the excess in salads.*

4 medium beets

1 avocado, chopped

1 lime, juiced

2 cups water

3 tablespoons hemp seeds

1 tablespoon ground coriander

¼ teaspoon sea salt

fresh cilantro leaves & black pepper, for garnish (optional)

First, roast the beets: heat the oven to 375° F and trim the beets, removing the stems and woody root. Individually wrap each beet in tin foil. Roast for 1 hour, or until tender, then let cool completely. Using a paper towel, rub off the beet skins. Trim away the ends, and chop the peeled beets coarsely. If making ahead of time, refrigerate until ready to use.

Place the beets, avocado, lime juice, water, hemp seeds, coriander, and sea salt in a blender. Blend until completely smooth. Place the soup into refrigerator, and chill for a minimum of 30 minutes. To serve, mix the soup well, and pour into serving bowls with a sprinkle of fresh cilantro and black pepper.

# GREENS SOUP

*This sophisticated soup practically glows—a hint of what it can offer your skin with its copious amounts of natural beauty-promoting vitamins and minerals, like vitamin C, vitamin E, silica, zinc, and much, much more. Note: English cucumbers are the smaller, sweeter, crisper cousins of our large "common" cucumbers. If you can't find them, don't sweat it—use regular cucumbers. Just make sure they're organic, as you'll be using the skin (where most of the nutrition is).*

6 cups English cucumbers, chopped

1 stalk celery, chopped

2 cups water

2 tablespoons fresh lime juice

1½ cups (packed) watercress leaves, plus ½ cup for garnish

¾ teaspoon sea salt

½ cup mashed avocado (about 1 avocado)

1 teaspoon freeze-dried wheatgrass powder

freshly cracked black pepper

Use a blender to puree the cucumbers, celery, water, lime juice, 1½ cups of the watercress, and sea salt together—blend as smooth as possible. Use a large, fine mesh sieve to strain the mixture and create a vibrant green broth. (Cheesecloth may also be used in place of a sieve; use a couple of layers to create a finer mesh.)

Return the broth to the blender and add the avocado and wheatgrass. Blend until smooth. Chill for a minimum of 30 minutes. To serve, garnish with a few watercress leaves and a little black pepper.

# STRAWBERRY SOUP

### MAKES 2–4 SERVINGS

*What a light and refreshing summer starter soup! I love this in conjunction with a big salad, or with one of the fresh zucchini "pastas" found in the Entreés section (page 115). Do note that strawberries are often one of the most heavily sprayed crops, so to avoid pesticides, choose organic (or grow your own).*

- 4 cups strawberries, stems removed
- ⅓ cup freshly squeezed orange juice
- 2 tablespoons fresh lemon zest
- chopped fresh mint leaves, for garnish (optional)

Blend all the ingredients except the mint together in a blender until smooth. Chill for a minimum of one hour, and garnish with mint just before serving.

**Variation:** For Acai-Strawberry Soup, increase the amount of orange juice to ⅔ cup, and add 2 tablespoons acai powder before blending.

## BENEFICIAL RAW SOUPS

Chilled (raw) fruit soups are more than just luxurious summer fare. They also offer something cooked soups often lack: vitamins and antioxidants. Since these health essentials are extra sensitive to heat, a lengthy stove top simmer doesn't do any favors to foods like berries, whose nutrients are found primarily in the vitamin and antioxidant categories. Raw soups, on the other hand, preserve every nutrient a food has to offer.

# TOMATO & QUINOA SOUP

*This recipe has always reminded me a bit of the alphabet soup I would eat as a kid. True, there may not be any letters to fish out, but if there were, they'd likely spell "healthy and fast." Of course, you can use freshly chopped vegetables here instead of frozen ones, but the latter makes this soup even easier and more convenient. Use your favorite organic vegetable blend, and make sure that the tomato paste has no added sweeteners—just tomatoes.*

⅓ cup tomato paste

6 cups water, divided

✺ 1 cup uncooked quinoa

3–4 cups frozen mixed vegetable blend (such as peas, carrots, corn, etc.)

3 tablespoons miso paste

Throw the tomato paste into a blender and add 5 cups of water. Blend for a quick moment to incorporate. Pour the mixture into a large pot and turn on the heat. Add the quinoa and frozen vegetables and bring to a boil. Cook for about 10–15 minutes or until quinoa is cooked through.

While the soup is cooking, pour the remaining 1 cup of water into the blender (no need to wash it out from the tomato mixture). Add the miso and quickly blend.

Once the quinoa is cooked through, turn off the heat. Stir in the miso mixture and serve hot.

**Serving Suggestion:** Top the finished soup with chopped avocado and a sprinkling of nutritional yeast.

# CARROT & YACON SOUP WITH GOJIS

*Since carrots and yacon are both "sweet" roots, they are natural flavor companions in this stunning, adventurous soup. Extra fun are the goji berries added at the end, which are pre-plumped in fresh carrot juice, and explode with sweet carrot flavor when chewed. Among its many benefits, this soup promotes healthy vision thanks to the high amounts of carotene in both the carrots and gojis, and supports good digestion because of the yacon.*

1½ cups fresh carrot juice

2 tablespoons dried goji berries

2 tablespoons coconut oil

1 cup sweet yellow onion, chopped

1 red jalapeño pepper, minced (seeds removed)

1 pound carrots, sliced into ¼-inch rounds

1 cup (packed) dried yacon slices

3 cups low-sodium vegetable broth

1 cup water

½ cup light coconut milk

sea salt and freshly cracked black pepper, to taste

edible flower petals and herbs, for garnish (optional)

In a small bowl or glass, mix the carrot juice and goji berries together. Let soak for 30 minutes, or until the berries are plump and soft.

While the berries are soaking, start the soup. Heat the coconut oil in a large pot over medium-high heat. Add the onions and sauté for 3–4 minutes to soften. Toss in the red jalapeño pepper, stir, and let cook for 1 minute longer. Add the carrots, yacon, vegetable broth, and water, then bring to a boil. Reduce the heat to a simmer, cover, and cook for 30 minutes, or until the carrots are soft. Transfer the mixture to a blender, add the coconut milk, and blend into a thick puree. Strain the goji berries from the carrot juice, setting the berries aside for a moment, and add the strained carrot juice to the soup. Blend until smooth. Adjust the salt and pepper to taste.

To serve, ladle the soup into bowls. Garnish with a few goji berries, an optional sprinkle of flower petals and herbs (like marigold petals and tarragon leaves), and a dusting of black pepper.

# BABY SPINACH &
# SEA BUCKTHORN BISQUE

MAKES 4 SERVINGS

*Rich yet light, this very special raw green soup has a purpose: beauty. A classic skin-rejuvenating berry, sea buckthorn offers special omegas and vitamin C for healthy tissue growth. In addition, avocado moisturizes the skin and spinach provides minerals and chlorophyll for enhancing circulation. Not bad for a soup . . .*

¼ cup raw cashews

2½ cups water

1½ medium avocados, peeled and pitted

3 cups baby spinach

1½ tablespoons fresh chives, minced

⅓ cup sea buckthorn juice

2 tablespoons miso paste

1 tablespoon lemon juice

1 teaspoon agave nectar

sea salt and black pepper, to taste

smoked paprika, for garnish

2 tablespoons mixed fresh herbs*, for garnish

*A mix of tarragon, parsley, and extra chives works well.

Combine the cashews and water in a blender and blend into a creamy milk. Add all the remaining ingredients, except the garnishes, and blend until smooth. Taste and adjust seasonings if necessary. Refrigerate for a minimum of 30 minutes, or until well chilled.

To serve, pour into small bowls and sprinkle lightly with paprika and fresh herbs.

# SALADS

*By no means is a salad only reserved for the side of a plate. Salads can be entire meals in themselves when stocked with nature's most powerful foods. Greens and sprouts are, of course, shoe-ins to include, but sea vegetables, healthy seeds and nuts, roots, and even fruits provide diversity in both nutrition and flavor. Plus, salad dressings offer the perfect vessel for potent superfood powders, which often hide in the background in terms of flavor, but are profoundly rewarding to the body.*

# SUSHI SALAD BOWL

MAKES 3–4 SERVINGS

*Even the most devout sushi lovers among us have lazy days, and this salad serves as the ideal remedy. No rolling, no assembling, no chopsticks—just simply toss and serve for instant sushi satisfaction. This filling salad easily functions as a complete meal, full of vital minerals and vitamins from the seaweed and sprouts.*

3½ cups cooked brown or wild rice, at room temperature

✴ 4 nori sheets

✴ 3 cups of sunflower sprouts, pea shoots, or other favorite sprouts

✴ 1 handful onion sprouts*

✴ 1 large avocado, peeled and cut into chunks

1 large carrot, grated

2 tablespoons sesame seeds

Ginger Dressing (page 107) or shoyu, to taste

*If onion sprouts are not available, substitute 2 finely sliced scallions.

Place the cooked rice in a large bowl. Stack the nori sheets, then use scissors to cut in half. Re-stack and cut in half again, lengthwise, forming long strips. Snip the strips widthwise into thin pieces and set aside for a moment. Add all of the vegetables to the rice and toss gently, then sprinkle in the nori and toss again. Make sure the nori is evenly distributed, or it will clump as it becomes soft. Sprinkle the sesame seeds on top and serve with Ginger Dressing or shoyu, or season as desired.

**Variation:** Add some cubed baked tofu or edamame to the mixture for an extra protein boost. Always buy organic soy products, as most conventionally grown soy is genetically modified.

# ARUGULA & ASIAN PEAR SALAD WITH LEMON-CAMU VINAIGRETTE

*Light and bright, this simple salad makes a lovely first course. The Asian pear acts almost like a sweet vegetable with its refreshing crispness, the chia seeds add texture and visual interest, and the lemony vinaigrette is the perfect complement to peppery arugula leaves.*

4 large handfuls of arugula leaves

1 large Asian pear, diced

1 tablespoon chia seeds

½ recipe Lemon-Camu Vinaigrette

In a large bowl, lightly toss the arugula and pear together with a little of the Lemon-Camu Vinaigrette, to taste. Transfer to serving plates, and sprinkle with chia seeds.

## LEMON-CAMU VINAIGRETTE

¼ cup fresh squeezed lemon juice

6 tablespoons EFA oil

2 teaspoons fresh lemon zest, finely minced

1 teaspoon camu powder

2 teaspoons agave nectar

1 teaspoon Dijon mustard

sea salt, to taste

Blend all the ingredients together until emulsified. Store up to 2 weeks, refrigerated; makes about ½ cup.

---

### SUPERFOOD TIP

In general, lemon juice serves as an excellent flavor mask for the camu berry's bitter flavor. This Lemon-Camu Vinaigrette gets a vitamin C boost of almost 1200 percent RDA thanks to the "secret" addition of this very special berry.

---

## LOCAL GREENS

Among the many benefits of salads is the opportunity to utilize locally grown produce, especially in the form of fresh leafy greens. Farmers' markets prove a particularly inspiring resource for finding new types of greens, which can instantly catapult a salad from boring to gourmet. Look for some of these special green (and red and purple) additions:

- Arugula/Rocket
- Baby Spinach
- Bibb/Butter Lettuce
- Chicory
- Claytonia
- Dandelion

- Endive
- Escarole
- Frisée
- Mache/Lamb's Lettuce
- Mesclun Mix
- Mizuna

- Oak Lettuce
- Purslane
- Radicchio
- Rainbow Chard
- Sorrel
- Watercress

# ROASTED VEGETABLE SALAD WITH BLACK PEPPER BALSAMIC VINAIGRETTE

MAKES 4 SERVINGS

*Tender roasted vegetables are balanced by crisp baby greens, then tossed with
a low-fat black pepper vinaigrette for a full-flavor salad that's filling yet light.*

2 tablespoons coconut oil

½ pound purple potatoes (or use fingerling or small red potatoes), quartered and cut into ½-inch thick slices

1–2 cloves garlic, minced

� 1 sprig rosemary, cut in half

2 medium zucchinis, cut into ½-inch cubes

½ medium eggplant, peeled, cut into ½-inch cubes

✦ 4 servings mixed baby greens (about 8–12 cups total)

1 recipe Black Pepper Balsamic Vinaigrette

sea salt and freshly cracked black pepper

Roast the vegetables first: Preheat the oven to 400° F, with a large roasting pan inside. Once the pan is hot, remove it from the oven and spread the coconut oil across the bottom. Toss together the potatoes, garlic, and rosemary in the pan, dressing well with the oil. Spread into a single, flat layer and put into the oven for 10 minutes. Remove the pan from the oven and add the zucchini, tossing to combine, then spread back into an even layer. Return the pan to the oven for another 5 minutes. Add the eggplant, season with salt and pepper, and toss again before finishing the roasting for 15 more minutes. Once fully cooked, let the roasted vegetables cool to room temperature before assembling the salad. Remove and discard the rosemary sprigs.

To serve, gently toss the baby greens with half of the Black Pepper Balsamic Vinaigrette in a large bowl, and arrange on serving plates. Top with a generous mound of roasted vegetables and drizzle the plate with a little additional dressing.

## BLACK PEPPER BALSAMIC VINAIGRETTE

2 tablespoons balsamic vinegar

2 tablespoons EFA oil

¼ cup apple juice

1 tablespoon freshly cracked black pepper

¼ teaspoon garlic powder

1 teaspoon Dijon mustard

✦ 1 teaspoon kelp powder

Mix all the vinaigrette ingredients. Makes slightly more than ½ cup.

# GODDESS KALE SALAD

MAKES 2–4 SERVINGS

*It's practically a law for health food stores to carry the irresistible salad dressing known as "Goddess Dressing." To date, I've never met a person who hasn't absolutely raved about it after a taste. My superfood version is indeed a tribute to this classic flavor, but has extra goddess-goodness with a detoxifying chlorella boost and beautifying hemp seeds. True: this dressing is undeniably green, but when tossed with the vibrant kale it blends right in. Frankly, I'd be happy putting this dressing on just about anything.*

1 bunch curly green kale
Superfood Goddess Dressing
⅔ cup cherry tomatoes, halved
2 tablespoons hemp seeds

### SUPERFOOD TIP
To easily separate kale leaves from the stem, hold a leaf by the thickest part of the stem. With the other hand, form a circle with your thumb and index finger, then slide this "ring" from the thick part of the stem to the thin, stripping off the leaves.

After washing the kale, make sure that the leaves are thoroughly dry. Remove and discard the thick parts of the stem from the kale leaves, and tear the leaves into large pieces. Put the kale into a big bowl. Add a few tablespoons of Superfood Goddess Dressing. Using clean hands, massage the dressing into the kale leaves, squeezing and tossing the leaves as you go to help soften them. Mix for about a minute, then add the cherry tomatoes and hemp seeds. Toss gently, taste, and add more dressing if needed.

### SUPERFOOD GODDESS DRESSING
3 tablespoons olive oil
2 tablespoons tahini
3 tablespoons water
3 tablespoons hemp seeds
1½ tablespoons apple cider vinegar
1 tablespoon lemon juice
2 teaspoons ume plum vinegar
1 teaspoon chlorella (or spirulina) powder
½ teaspoon garlic powder
¼ teaspoon onion powder
¼ teaspoon kelp powder (optional)

Blend all ingredients together until smooth. Store in the refrigerator when not in use; will keep up to 2 weeks. Makes about ¾ cup.

# SIMPLE SPINACH SALAD WITH MULBERRY-MUSTARD DRESSING

MAKES 4 SERVINGS

*Mulberries are so beautifully sweet, they can stand in for the syrup or honey that would normally be used in a sweet mustard dressing (which also happens to be fat-free). Tossed with iron-rich spinach, crisp pickled onions, creamy avocado, and crunchy EFA-rich flax seeds, this salad is a nutritionally balanced pleasure.*

8 large handfuls baby spinach
Mulberry-Mustard Dressing
½ cup Quick Pickled Onions (see page 104)
1 avocado, pitted, peeled, and cut into chunks
3 tablespoons flaxseeds

In a large bowl, gently toss the spinach and several spoonfuls of the Mulberry-Mustard Dressing with clean hands to evenly coat the leaves. Transfer the salad to serving plates, and top with the onions, avocado, and flaxseeds.

## MULBERRY-MUSTARD DRESSING

⅔ cup dried mulberries
3 tablespoons Dijon mustard
½ cup apple juice
2 tablespoons apple cider vinegar

In a blender (use a small one if you have it), blend the mulberries, mustard, apple juice, and apple cider vinegar into a smooth consistency. Keep covered and refrigerated when not in use; will last for a few weeks. Makes about 1 cup.

# CABBAGE-POMEGRANATE SLAW

MAKES 3–4 SERVINGS

*This sweet and tangy slaw really pops with the addition of pomegranate seeds.*
*Serve as a light side salad, and enjoy the antioxidant-rich rainbow.*

4 cups green cabbage, shredded

2 carrots, grated

⅓ cup Quick Pickled Onions
    (page 104)

❋ 1 cup pomegranate seeds

1 tablespoon EFA oil

❋ 2 tablespoons yacon syrup

1 tablespoon fresh lime juice

1 teaspoon Dijon mustard

½ teaspoon sea salt

Toss the cabbage, carrots, onions, and pomegranate in a large bowl. In a small bowl, mix together the oil, yacon syrup, lime juice, mustard, and salt. Pour the mixture over the vegetables, and toss well. Slaw may be enjoyed right away, but is best when given the opportunity to marinate in the refrigerator for an hour or two.

### SUPERFOOD TIP

Pomegranate seeds are a wonderful addition to salads, and pair especially well with "heavier" leafy greens like cabbage, kale, spinach, and chard. They add complimentary flavor and texture without being overwhelmingly sweet.

# HEARTY KALE SALAD

*Ranking at the very top of the nutrient density charts, there's a reason why eating kale feels so, so good. Here, combined with mineral-rich nori and skin-healthy fats from the avocado, this salad is essentially the definition of "balanced energy." I like to make it a meal, served with baked sweet potato fries. Try this combination and you may never want to eat anything less delicious again.*

- 1 big bunch of green kale, washed, dried, and stems removed
- 1½ medium avocados, peeled and pitted
- 1½ tablespoons miso paste
- 3 scallions, very thinly sliced—white and light green parts only
- 2 tablespoons apple cider vinegar
- 3 sheets nori, cut with kitchen scissors into thin strips (optional)

Tear the kale by hand into bite-size pieces and place in a large bowl.

In a small bowl, mash one of the avocados with the miso paste, scallions, and vinegar into a chunky guacamole-like mixture. Spoon into the bowl with the kale. Using clean hands, massage the avocado mixture into the kale, squeezing and tossing the leaves, for about 2 minutes. Chop the remaining ½ avocado into chunks and scatter over the salad. Sprinkle the nori (if desired) and toss thoroughly.

### SUPERFOOD TIP

"Massaging" kale is a smart (and secretly rather fun) technique that helps wilt the leaves, similar to cooking. It increases digestibility while ensuring the maximum amount of nutrients are retained by keeping the vegetables raw.

## QUICK PICKLED ONIONS

*Beautifully fuschia-colored, this quick accompaniment has a way of glorifying any dish. The simple brine pickles the onion slices, enhancing the crispness and making the onions more mild and sweet.*

1 red onion, sliced as thinly as possible
2 cups apple cider vinegar
½ teaspoon sea salt

Place the onion slices into a quart-size mason jar. Pour the vinegar on top, and add the salt. Close the jar tightly and give it a good shake for 30 seconds. Press the onions back down until everything is submerged in the vinegar solution, and let rest for 10 minutes. Drain the vinegar, and squeeze the onions to remove any excess moisture.

# CALIFORNIA SALAD

*This salad is my mom's culinary claim-to-fame, and with good reason. She takes advantage of the plethora of fresh vegetables grown around her SoCal seaside home to make what is otherwise known (by everyone who's tried it) as simply "THE Salad." It's exceptional, and I won't blame you if you never want to eat a different salad again. Every time I visit her, there's always a giant bowl of this waiting in the fridge. (And by the time I leave, it's gone).*

- ½ pound Romaine lettuce, chopped
- ¼ pound mixed baby greens
- ¼ pound arugula
- ¼ pound sunflower sprouts (or your favorite sprouts)
- 2 cups fresh corn kernels
- 1 red bell pepper, seeds removed, diced
- ½ large English cucumber, unpeeled, cut into quarter rounds
- 1 cup sweet cherry tomatoes, halved
- 1½ avocados, peeled and cut into cubes
- California Dressing

In a large bowl, toss the lettuce, baby greens, arugula, and sprouts together. Layer the remaining ingredients on top, and serve "family style" with California Dressing on the side for self-serving.

## CALIFORNIA DRESSING

- ¼ cup EFA oil
- 3 tablespoons ume plum vinegar
- 1 tablespoon shoyu
- ¼ cup apple cider vinegar
- 1 tablespoon fresh rosemary, minced
- ½ teaspoon dried oregano
- 1 teaspoon garlic powder
- 1 teaspoon onion powder
- 1 teaspoon black pepper
- 1 teaspoon kelp powder (optional)

Mix all ingredients until combined. Store in the refrigerator when not in use; will keep for about 2 weeks. Makes close to ⅔ cup.

# SPRINGTIME SALAD WITH GINGER DRESSING

## MAKES 4–6 SERVINGS

*A good salad is easy to make, as proven by this light, fresh, and visually stunning combination. Soaking the goji berries makes them juicy while also diluting their flavor, resulting in a taste that borders on a sweet cherry tomato. Feel free to add or substitute your favorite in-season vegetables here—there are very few rules in salad-making.*

※ ¼ cup dried goji berries

   1 cup hot water

※ 1 pound mixed greens

※ ¼ pound sunflower sprouts (or other variety of sprouts)

   6 English Breakfast radishes (or other mild radish), thinly sliced

※ a few pinches of minced fresh garden herbs (such as thyme, tarragon, basil, etc.)

   edible garden flowers (such as carnations, pansies, marigolds, etc.), optional

   Ginger Dressing

Place the goji berries into a small bowl or glass and pour the hot water over them. Steep for 30 minutes or longer, until the goji berries are plump. Strain the berries for the salad (and reserve the soak water for yourself to enjoy later—it makes a lovely cup of tea).

In a large salad bowl, toss the greens, sunflower sprouts, radishes, soaked goji berries, and herbs together. When ready to serve, gently toss with as much Ginger Dressing as desired, using your fingertips to mix together to avoid bruising the greens. Sprinkle with flower petals for decoration, if desired, and serve immediately.

### GINGER DRESSING:

½ cup apple juice

2 tablespoons miso paste

2 tablespoons peeled fresh ginger root, minced

2 large Medjool dates, pits removed

1 tablespoon + 1 teaspoon apple cider vinegar

Blend all ingredients together until smooth. Makes ⅔ cup. Will keep for about 1 week when refrigerated.

# SUPERFRUIT SALAD

MAKES ABOUT 6 SERVINGS

*When a fruit salad tastes this good, getting a full day's ration of fresh produce in just one sitting is almost inevitable. This recipe is flexible enough to accommodate in-season fruits—feel free to improvise!—but try to keep the superberries in. The dried goji berries and goldenberries will soften as the fruit marinates, soaking up the juices from the fruits, and making them especially delicious.*

3 cups pineapple, cut into 1-inch cubes

⅔ cup dried goldenberries

½ cup dried goji berries

3 cups strawberries, quartered

1 cup blueberries

3 cups green grapes, halved

2 cups apples, cut into 1-inch cubes

1 cup pomegranate seeds

2 tablespoons agave nectar, or yacon syrup

1 teaspoon vanilla extract

Combine all the fruits in a large bowl. In a small glass, mix together the agave and vanilla. Pour over the fruit and toss gently. Cover, and refrigerate for a minimum of two hours to let the flavors marry. Toss before serving. Will last for several days, refrigerated.

# BUTTER LETTUCE SALAD WITH CREAMY SEA BUCKTHORN DRESSING

## MAKES 6 APPETIZER SERVINGS

*Sea buckthorn's unusual flavor punch lends itself extremely well to salad dressings, providing a yogurt-like flavor to this deceptively simple recipe. I find this dressing so delicious that I can eat it on butter lettuce and not add a thing. If your table is dressed to impress, however, the full recipe below offers a starter salad that will turn even the most questioning palates into superfood converts.*

- 2 heads butter lettuce, washed and dried
- ½ cup jicama, peeled and diced into ¼-inch cubes
- 6 tablespoons pistachios, shells removed
- 6 tablespoons dried goldenberries
- Creamy Sea Buckthorn Dressing, to taste

Gently tear the butter lettuce into large pieces and place in a large bowl. Drizzle and toss with as much dressing as desired, then transfer to serving plates. Distribute the jicama, pistachios, and goldenberries evenly among the plates and serve.

### CREAMY SEA BUCKTHORN DRESSING

- ⅓ cup sea buckthorn juice
- ½ cup water
- ½ cup raw cashews
- 2 teaspoons white miso paste
- ½ teaspoon fresh thyme, chopped
- ½ teaspoon sea salt
- ¼ teaspoon black pepper

Combine all the ingredients in a small blender, and blend until thoroughly smooth. Makes 1¼ cups.

# MIZUNA, FENNEL & MULBERRY SALAD

*Mizuna is a Japanese green leafy vegetable that tastes like a mild form of arugula, and is fast becoming the new leafy green darling of farmers' markets and some natural food stores (if unavailable, arugula will make a fine substitute). Incredibly, the fresh combination of natural ingredients is so flavorful in this salad, barely any dressing is needed!*

1 large fennel bulb, including fronds

2 tablespoons fresh lemon juice

2 tablespoons olive oil

1½ tablespoons fennel seeds

½ teaspoon sea salt

½ teaspoon freshly cracked black pepper, or to taste

✳ 1 large bunch mizuna, stems trimmed and removed

✳ ¼ cup chopped fresh parsley

✳ ⅔ cup dried mulberries

Trim off the fennel root and fronds, leaving a 1-inch handle on top of the bulb. Reserve the fronds. Use a mandolin to carefully shave the fennel bulb into paper-thin slices, yielding around 6 cups. Fill a large bowl with water and ice and place the fennel in the bath for about 10 minutes to crisp.

In a small bowl, whisk together the lemon juice, olive oil, fennel seeds, sea salt, and black pepper to form a simple dressing.

When the fennel is crisp, remove the shavings from the ice bath and drain thoroughly. Gently pat dry with towels to remove any excess moisture, and place in a large bowl along with the mizuna, parsley, and ⅓ cup mulberries. Toss to combine, add the dressing, and gently mix by hand to distribute the ingredients evenly. To serve, place in serving bowls, then top with remaining mulberries and a few small sprigs of the reserved fennel fronds. Add additional black pepper if desired.

# ENTRÉES

*When you think about it, so many of the foods we enjoy are based on the same food structures, over and over again (e.g. how many lasagna recipes are there in the world?). That's because familiarity itself is an important culinary element. Nonetheless, introducing new ingredients within the regular "architecture" of our favorite foods is where superfoods really shine. They're quick and energizing subs for the old tired hats of the kitchen—like risotto made from quinoa, large savory leaves used like tortillas, or hemp seeds acting as a tantalizing new type of "meat." And yes, there's even a superfood lasagna.*

# CHIPOTLE CHILI WITH AVOCADO SOUR CREAM

## MAKES 4 SERVINGS

*You'd never guess this savory chili contains healthy wakame in it since it almost melts away while cooking, leaving only its minerals and detoxifying benefits behind. Like most good chilis, this recipe loves a nice, slow cook to allow the flavors to meld, but is definitely worth the wait.*

6 cups chopped tomatoes, divided

2 tablespoons coconut oil

1 medium yellow onion, diced

4 cloves garlic, minced

2 stalks celery, diced

2 fresh Anaheim peppers, diced

1 lb sweet potatoes, peeled and diced

1 tablespoon fresh thyme leaves, chopped

1 teaspoon chipotle powder

4 cups cooked black beans (unsalted)

2 heaping tablespoons wakame flakes

3 cups vegetable broth

sea salt, to taste

Avocado Sour Cream

### SUPERFOOD TIP
In many parts of Asia, cooking beans with seaweed is a common practice. Aside from enhancing the beans' flavor and texture, seaweed also assists in neutralizing the notorious enzyme in beans that can lead to gas.

Blend 4 cups of the tomatoes in a blender or food processor until a chunky puree has formed. Set aside.

In a large pot, melt the coconut oil over medium-high heat. Add the onions and sauté until softened, about 5 minutes. Add the garlic, celery, peppers, and sweet potato, plus the remaining 2 cups of chopped tomatoes and sauté for about 5 minutes longer to help break down the tomatoes. Add the prepared tomato puree, thyme, chipotle, cooked beans, wakame, and vegetable broth to the pot. Season with some salt, stir to combine, and bring to a boil. Reduce the heat to low, cover, and simmer for 45 minutes. Taste and add additional salt if needed, then simmer over low heat, uncovered, for 15 minutes longer, adding a little water if necessary. When the chili is finished cooking, serve hot, with a dollop of Avocado Sour Cream.

## AVOCADO SOUR CREAM

⅔ cup raw cashews

⅔ cup water

1 large avocado (preferably Hass variety), pitted and peeled

2 tablespoons fresh lime juice

½ teaspoon sea salt

Use a small blender to process the cashews and water together into a smooth cream. Add the avocado, lime juice, and sea salt, then blend again to form a whip. Refrigerate until ready to use. Will keep for several days in a sealed container, refrigerated.

# ZUCCHINI FETTUCCINE WITH WALNUTS & DULSE

## MAKES 2–4 SERVINGS

*I love the combination of walnuts and dulse: rich, salty, and a little meaty. This simple dish really celebrates the full flavor of dulse and is very lightly cooked . . . just enough to get the job done. I serve it as a main course where, somehow, it feels like it belongs amongst the great family of classic Italian dishes.*

8 medium zucchini

1 teaspoon sea salt

2 tablespoons coconut oil

2 cups diced yellow onion (about one large onion)

⅔ cup packed dulse strips, torn into 1-inch pieces

½ cup chopped walnuts

¼ cup fresh minced parsley, plus a little extra for garnish

### SUPERFOOD TIP

Avoid using dulse flakes in place of the dulse strips here. The strip-form helps control the seaweed's umami flavor so the dish does not become overpowered by it. Dulse flakes are a wonderful ingredient to have on hand in the kitchen, but are better used as a topping style of seasoning.

Using a handheld vegetable peeler, carefully strip the zucchini, layer by layer, into noodle-like ribbons—avoid/discard the center section that holds the watery seeds. Toss the zucchini strips with sea salt and place in a colander. Rest over a large bowl to catch excess moisture, and let stand for 30 minutes.

After 30 minutes, wash the zucchini noodles thoroughly with warm water to remove the excess salt, squeeze lightly to remove a little moisture, and let drain thoroughly. Set aside.

Heat the coconut oil in a large skillet over medium-high heat. Add the onions and sauté until they have softened and begun to turn translucent, about 5–6 minutes. Toss in the dulse, walnuts, and parsley and cook for 2 minutes longer—the dulse will quickly change color as it cooks. Lastly, add the zucchini noodles, tossing everything together, and cook until the zucchini is just warmed through and has turned bright green—about 1–2 minutes. Do not overcook. Remove from heat, season with salt and pepper if desired, and toss with remaining parsley to serve.

**Variation:** Use quinoa noodles instead of the zucchini.

# QUINOA SPAGHETTI WITH CASHEW CREAM SAUCE & CHARD

### MAKES 4 SERVINGS

*Quinoa spaghetti—made out of organic milled quinoa and corn—is an exciting alternative to traditional (nutrient-void) pasta varieties. Along with being gluten-free, this superfood pasta contains protein, offers plentiful minerals, and tastes great. I love it in this fresh combination featuring copious amounts of delicious green chard and a savory cashew cream sauce. A tip: Do an extra good job of cleaning your swiss chard—it can be sandy.*

- 2 large bunches swiss chard, cleaned thoroughly
- 2 cups water
- ⅔ cup raw cashews
- ½ teaspoon sea salt
- 1 teaspoon fresh lemon zest
- 1 8-ounce package quinoa spaghetti
- 2 tablespoons coconut oil
- ½ cup minced shallots (about 2 or 3)
- freshly cracked black pepper, to taste

Prep a few of the ingredients first: Cut the thick stems off the end of the chard leaves and discard. Slice the leaves into ½-inch strips by stacking a few chard leaves on top of one another, then rolling into a fat cigar-like shape before slicing. Next, blend the water, cashews, salt, and lemon zest together into a smooth cream. Set these ingredients aside for a moment.

Cook the quinoa pasta according to the manufacturer's directions.

A few minutes before the quinoa pasta is ready, warm the coconut oil over medium heat in a large pan. Add the shallots and sauté for a minute—just long enough to let the shallots lightly caramelize and begin to turn golden. Add the chard, toss well, then reduce the heat to medium-low and cover. Cook for 4–5 minutes, or until the chard's color turns vibrant and the leaves are wilted. Remove the cover and pour in the blended creamy sauce. Cook, stirring, for 1–2 minutes to warm the sauce. Drain the pasta and combine with the chard mixture, tossing thoroughly to distribute the ingredients. Season with freshly cracked black pepper to taste, and serve warm.

# CAULIFLOWER RISOTTO

MAKES 2–4 SERVINGS

*Sneaky, sneaky: Instead of the notoriously heavy risottos of many a restaurant's fame, this recipe uses finely ground cauliflower to act like an enticingly moist rice, mixed in with fluffy quinoa for a nice textural agent and protein boost. This risotto is excellent for foodies looking to cut calories, for while the portions may appear large in size, much of the bulk is attributed to the cauliflower, which is a very low-calorie food.*

1 medium leek

1 medium head of cauliflower

1 tablespoon coconut oil, divided

2 cloves garlic, minced

1½ tablespoons tahini

1 tablespoon nutritional yeast

1 tablespoon miso paste

1½ cups vegetable broth

※ 1½ cups cooked quinoa

½ tablespoon lemon juice

※ ¼ cup hemp seeds

※ ½ tablespoon dulse flakes (optional)

sea salt and freshly cracked black pepper, to taste

※ 1 – 2 tablespoons chopped fresh parsley

Cut the end roots off of the leek and trim to the white part only, then slice in half lengthwise. Place the halves cut-side down in a small bowl of water for a few minutes to remove any sand. Remove the cleaned leeks and slice thinly. Next, trim the cauliflower to the florets and discard the fibrous stem. Place the florets into a food processor and mill into tiny pieces (about the size of rice). Set the vegetables aside.

In a large frying pan, heat about ½ tablespoon coconut oil over medium heat. Add the leeks and the garlic, and sauté for 2 minutes to wilt the leeks. Stir in the cauliflower, then cook the mixture for about 5 minutes to remove some of the moisture and soften, stirring occasionally. While the cauliflower is cooking, whisk together the tahini, nutritional yeast, miso paste, and vegetable broth in a medium bowl.

When the cauliflower is cooked through, add the quinoa and pour in the whisked vegetable broth mixture. Mix well. Bring the risotto to a simmer and cook until all the excess liquid has evaporated, about 5 minutes. Remove from heat, stir in the lemon juice, hemp seeds, remaining ½ tablespoon coconut oil, and dulse (if desired). Season to taste with sea salt and black pepper. Sprinkle the parsley on top and serve warm.

# KABOCHA-QUINOA RISOTTO WITH SAGE CREAM & SUN-DRIED YACON ROOT

*Kabocha is a rising star in the winter squash world, as its rich orange flesh is hard to beat in terms of sweet flavor and melt-away texture. Its inherent creaminess works as an epic base for a risotto like this one, which uses quinoa for extra nutrition instead of the traditional risotto rice. Yacon root is used to flavor the Sage Cream, and adds a wonderfully sweet, almost smoky element, as a chewy addition on top. Luckily for us, yacon root is sold sun-dried, so this gourmet facade is actually as simple as opening a bag.*

- 1 cup uncooked (dry) quinoa
- 4 cups vegetable stock, divided
- 1 tablespoon coconut oil
- 2 cups kabocha squash, peeled, seeded, and cut into ½-inch cubes
- ¼ teaspoon sea salt
- freshly cracked black pepper, to taste
- ¼ teaspoon ground nutmeg
- ¾ cup Sweet Sage Cream (page 159)
- ½ cup (packed) dried yacon slices
- 2 tablespoons chopped fresh parsley, for garnish

### SUPERFOOD TIP
Dicing vegetables like hard winter squash can be quickly accomplished using a food processor to save time.

Rinse the quinoa with water and place into a medium saucepan. Pour in 2½ cups of the vegetable stock, cover the pan, and bring to a boil over medium-high heat. Remove the cover and turn down the heat to reduce the contents to a simmer. Cook for 15 minutes, or until quinoa is cooked through and translucent (quinoa will appear a little more watery and soft than usual). Cover and keep warm.

While the quinoa is cooking, prepare the squash: Heat the coconut oil over medium heat in a large nonstick pan. Add the diced kabocha, ½ cup vegetable stock, sea salt, and some freshly cracked black pepper. Cook until squash is soft, about 5–8 minutes. Add the nutmeg and cook 1 minute longer. Remove from heat, transfer to a food processor, and puree until smooth.

In a large saucepan, combine the cooked quinoa, squash puree, remaining ¾ cup vegetable stock, and ½ cup Sweet Sage Cream; cook over low heat for 2–3 minutes, until heated through. Adjust salt and pepper to taste, and add additional vegetable stock as needed. To serve, divide risotto onto serving plates, swirl in a little extra Sweet Sage Cream on top, plant several yacon slices in the risotto bed, and sprinkle with parsley.

# WATERCRESS MOCHI PIZZA

### MAKES 3 SINGLE-SERVING PIZZAS

*Mochi is a Japanese stroke of brilliant food-making; it's a type of sticky brown rice that's mashed together so that when you cook it, the mochi puffs up, like a cross between a biscuit and a muffin. I love the simplicity of mochi—it's traditionally composed of rice: no more, no less. Thinly sliced, it makes the most delectable pizza crust, topped here with a white sauce and a leafy-green superfood extraordinaire: peppery watercress. Best when cut and served fresh off the stove, it is a phenomenal appetizer, but is filling enough for a main course as well. You can't help but get excited when a homemade pizza takes just about 15 minutes to make from start to finish.*

1 package brown rice mochi
(12.5 ounces)

2 cups watercress leaves

1 – 2 tablespoons Lemon-Camu
Vinaigrette (page 96)

⅓ cup cashews

¾ cup water

1 large clove garlic, minced

¼ teaspoon sea salt

coconut oil, for cooking

freshly ground black pepper, to taste

Prep a few ingredients first: Cut the mochi into ¼-inch, thin, long strips and set aside. In a medium bowl, lightly toss the watercress with Lemon-Camu Vinaigrette and cover until ready to use.

Blend together the cashews, water, garlic, and sea salt into a smooth cream (strain through a fine mesh sieve if needed/desired to remove any particulates that are not fully blended). Pour into a small saucepan, and bring to a simmer over low heat. Continue to gently simmer, stirring frequently to avoid burning, until the cream has reduced by about half to form a thick white sauce—about 5 minutes. Remove from heat and cover to keep warm.

For each personal pizza (recipe makes 3), heat a small amount of coconut oil over medium-low heat in a nonstick frying pan. To properly form the pizza crust, take 8 mochi strips and lay them in the pan, one at a time, so they are close together but not touching (like stripes). Working quickly, use a spatula to nudge the edges so they are flush, then slide the strips together so that they are all touching lengthwise, forming an even square. Let cook for about 5 minutes, or until the bottom is lightly browned and the mochi has begun to puff up, then flip the mochi over (the strips should stick together as one square). Spoon about a third of the white sauce over the surface of the cooked side, and continue to cook for another 3–4 minutes or until the bottom is golden. Remove from heat, and slice into quarters, topping each square with watercress and black pepper.

# MEDITERRANEAN VEGETABLE PIZZA

## MAKES 1 PIZZA (4 SERVINGS)

*This is a pizza more by architecture than by detail. The crust is a high-protein, cracker-like flatbread boosted with super seeds; the sauce is a savory olive spread rich in minerals and healthy fats; and the vibrant topping boasts copious amounts of flavorful cooked vegetables. A note: Since the pizza dough does not rise, be sure to roll it thinly enough so that it bakes nice and crispy!*

### FOR THE CRUST

½ cup brown rice flour, plus a little extra for dusting

¼ cup flaxseed powder

½ teaspoon sea salt

¼ teaspoon garlic powder

1½ cups cooked garbanzo beans, unsalted

2 tablespoons tahini

2 tablespoons water

1 tablespoon chia seeds, divided
olive oil, for baking

### FOR THE PIZZA TOPPING

1 – 2 tablespoons olive oil

½ red onion, thinly sliced

2 cloves garlic, minced

1 cup portabello mushrooms, chopped into ½-inch cubes

1 cup cherry tomatoes, halved
sea salt, to taste

4 cups (packed) spinach leaves

1 batch Olive Caviar (page 156)
red pepper flakes, to taste

First, make the crust: Mix the flour, flaxseed powder, salt, and garlic powder together in a small bowl. In a food processor, blend the garbanzo beans, tahini, water, and 1 teaspoon of the chia seeds into a smooth paste. Add in the dry mixture and process again to form a dough. Form the dough into a compact ball and let rest, covered, for 15 minutes.

Preheat the oven to 375° F, and prepare the surface of a cookie sheet with a light rub of coconut or olive oil. Lay a few overlapping pieces of wax paper on a countertop to cover a large rolling area, and lightly dust the surface with brown rice flour. Place the dough on top. Dust a rolling pin with more flour, and roll the dough into an ⅛-inch layer to fit the size of your baking sheet, reshaping and patching rolled areas as needed. Leave the edges rough, or trim if desired. Sprinkle the remaining chia seeds on top and use your fingers to press the seeds into the dough. To transfer the dough to the cookie sheet, lay the sheet face down on top of the dough. Slide one hand underneath the wax paper, and place the other hand on top of the baking sheet. Quickly flip the two over, and peel away the wax paper. Bake for 20 minutes.

Meanwhile, make the pizza topping. Heat a tablespoon of olive oil in a medium sauté pan. Add the onions, and cook for 3–4 minutes, then add the garlic, mushrooms, tomatoes, and a little sea salt for seasoning. Cook for another 3–4 minutes, add the spinach, and turn off the heat. Toss the vegetables in the hot pan to wilt the spinach and combine the flavors. When the crust is ready, remove from the oven and evenly spread the Olive Caviar on the crust. Top with the vegetable mixture and return to the oven. Bake for 10 more minutes. To serve, sprinkle with red pepper flakes and cut into slices with a pizza roller.

# ZUCCHINI FETTUCCINE WITH MEGA MARINARA

## MAKES 4 SERVINGS

*This is a great recipe to serve in the peak of summertime, as it not only makes use of vibrant warm-weather produce, but it can also be served as a delicious raw dish if desired, so you don't even have to turn on the stove. However, quickly heating it makes for a very comforting dish . . . I'd be hard pressed to pick which version I like better.*

12 medium zucchini

1 teaspoon sea salt

1 cup walnuts, divided

2 cups cherry tomatoes

3 tablespoons dried goji berries

¼ cup raisins

¼ cup (packed) chopped fresh basil

2 teaspoons fresh oregano, minced

1 teaspoon fresh garlic, minced

1 tablespoon miso paste

½ teaspoon kelp powder (optional)

⅓ cup hemp seeds

---

**SUPERFOOD TIP**

Replacing pasta with ribbons of zucchini (which act like noodles) is an excellent way to cut calories and increase nutrient density. Pre-salting the ribbons tenderizes them, but don't be alarmed by the salt content—most of it is washed away.

---

Use a vegetable peeler to strip the zucchini into ribbons, avoiding the watery core that holds the seeds. Set the ribbons into a colander and toss with the salt. Set over a plate to drain for 30 minutes.

Meanwhile, place the walnuts in a food processor. Pulse into small pieces, remove, and set aside for later. Place the tomatoes, goji berries, raisins, basil, oregano, garlic, miso paste, and kelp into the processor and blend into a smooth paste. Stop the machine and scrape the sides down if needed to make sure everything gets incorporated. Add 2 tablespoons of the walnuts and blend again. If sauce is too thick (depending upon the juiciness of the tomatoes), add a tablespoon or two of water. Transfer the sauce to a bowl, and fold in the remaining walnuts and hemp seeds.

Wash off the zucchini ribbons thoroughly to remove the excess salt, and gently squeeze out the extra water. Complete the dish using one of the following methods below:

**Raw method (cold):** Transfer the zucchini to serving plates, top with the sauce and serve. May also be pre-warmed in a dehydrator.

**Cooked method (hot):** Place the zucchini in a pan with a teaspoon of coconut oil. Cook over low heat until warm to the touch, about 2 minutes. Add the sauce and cook for just a minute or two longer to get everything nice and hot. Serve immediately.

# NORI-BEAN LETTUCE WRAPS

## MAKES 8 WRAPS (ABOUT 4 SERVINGS)

*These filling wraps can be eaten just like a taco. The nori bean pâté is reminiscent of tuna salad in flavor and nutrition, providing EFAs and a high-protein content, but avoiding the threat of heavy metal toxicity that accompanies many fish. A fabulous main course for lunch or a light dinner.*

1 tablespoon ume plum vinegar

2 tablespoons sesame seeds

2 cups cooked brown rice

1 batch Nori-Bean Pâté

1 avocado, pitted, peeled, and cut into 8 slices

8–10 red or butter lettuce leaves

Mix the ume plum vinegar and sesame seeds with the cooked brown rice in a bowl. To assemble the lettuce cups, lay a lettuce leaf on a flat surface. Add a few tablespoons of the rice mixture in the center, and smear a scoop of the Nori-Bean Pâté on top. Add an avocado strip, then roll up like soft taco. Repeat with the remaining leaves and serve as a finger food.

### NORI-BEAN PÂTÉ

4 cups cooked garbanzo beans

8 raw nori sheets

2 teaspoons shallots, minced

3 tablespoons shoyu

¼ cup EFA oil

2 tablespoons fresh lime juice

2 stalks celery, minced

With the back of a fork, mash the garbanzo beans into a chunky paste. Crumble the nori sheets into fine flakes, and sprinkle into the mashed beans. Mix thoroughly, then add the remaining ingredients until combined. Refrigerate until ready to use.

### SUPERFOOD TIP

When selecting lettuce or greens for wraps, be sure to inspect the produce for quality, looking for leaves that appear in good condition without any (or at least minimal) holes or tears. If your lettuce leaves aren't in top shape, simply double up two leaves per wrap to avoid the filling contents inside from messily spilling out.

# POMEGRANATE-GLAZED PORTABELLO STEAKS OVER LEMONY SPINACH

### MAKES 4 SERVINGS

*The pomegranate's complex sweet-acidic dichotomy complements the earthy meatiness of the portabello, providing a very balanced flavor profile. A truly elegant dish that goes well with a favorite red wine.*

## FOR THE GLAZE

- 1 cup pomegranate juice
- 1 tablespoon coconut sugar
- 1 tablespoon red wine vinegar
- ½ teaspoon fresh thyme leaves, chopped
- ¼ teaspoon sea salt
- ½ tablespoon coconut oil

## FOR THE PORTABELLO STEAKS

- ¼ cup olive oil
- ⅓ cup red wine
- 1 teaspoon red pepper flakes
- 1 tablespoon pressed garlic
- ½ teaspoon sea salt
- 4 portabello mushrooms
- 2 pounds spinach leaves
- 1 lemon
- sea salt and freshly cracked pepper, to taste
- ½ cup pomegranate seeds
- handful microgreens or sprouts, for garnish

Make the glaze first: In a small saucepan, combine all the glaze ingredients and bring to a boil. Reduce the heat to a simmer, and cook for 20 minutes to reduce into a thick sauce. Set aside.

In a small bowl, whisk together the oil, red wine, red pepper flakes, garlic, and salt—you can also use a small blender to better emulsify. Snap the stems off of the portabello caps and discard or save for another recipe. Brush both sides of each mushroom cap thoroughly with the marinade. Heat a large nonstick pan over medium heat and place the mushrooms inside, ribbed side facing up. Pour any remaining marinade over the mushrooms in the pan. Cook until the mushrooms are soft, about 5–7 minutes, flipping halfway through cooking.

While the mushrooms are cooking, wilt the spinach by either steaming lightly, or simply heating in a separate nonstick pan for a minute or two until just wilted. Toss with the juice of one lemon and season with salt and pepper to taste.

To assemble, place a bed of spinach on four plates. Slice each mushroom if desired, or leave whole and set on top of the spinach. Drizzle the top with the pomegranate glaze, then sprinkle with pomegranate seeds and microgreens or sprouts.

# ASIAN TEMPEH LETTUCE CUPS

## MAKES 2–4 SERVINGS (AS A MAIN COURSE)

*Who needs a tortilla, anyway? Cool, crispy lettuce does the "wrap" job well, while also balancing the warmth of the tempeh filling. These lettuce cups are great for a casual lunch, or can be made into a more substantial meal by simply adding an extra side of warm brown rice or quinoa. The filling can even be made ahead of time and brought as a potluck dish, with the lettuce offered on the side for self-serve-style enjoyment.*

1 tablespoon wakame flakes

1 teaspoon coriander powder

1 teaspoon pressed fresh garlic

2 tablespoons shoyu

2 tablespoons coconut oil

8 ounces tempeh, cut into ½-inch cubes

¼ cup raw cashews, coarsely chopped

1 green onion, thinly sliced

1 cup mung bean sprouts

¼ cup fresh cilantro leaves

8–10 butter lettuce leaves

Soak the wakame flakes in a glass of warm water for 20 minutes to soften. Drain and set aside until ready to use. While the wakame is soaking, mix together the coriander, pressed garlic, and shoyu in a small bowl. Set aside.

Warm the coconut oil over medium heat in a medium-size skillet. Add the tempeh, and cook for 8–10 minutes, tossing occasionally, until the tempeh is golden brown on all sides.

Remove the pan from the heat and immediately add in the cashews, green onion, wakame, and shoyu mixture. Stir quickly to incorporate thoroughly for about 30 seconds, then add the mung bean sprouts and cilantro and toss well. Transfer to a serving bowl.

To serve, place a couple of spoonfuls of the warm stir-fry mixture into an open lettuce leaf cup. Loosely wrap and eat like a soft taco.

### SUPERFOOD TIP

Tempeh ("tem-pay") is a cultured soy or grain product (a whole food), similar to a highly dense vegetable burger. Some companies are now making unique tempeh blends which include star ingredients flax, hemp, or seaweed. If available, choose these superfood-infused upgrades and take advantage of the extra nutrition.

# LOADED COLLARD WRAPS

## MAKES 4 WRAPS

*I love this recipe because it is so, so versatile. The basic concept is taking a large leaf and using it like a tortilla, then stuffing the wrap with veggies galore and flavorful spreads. I've included my favorite combination of veggies and spreads for this ultra-loaded recipe, but improvisation is perhaps the best ingredient off all. One indispensable secret used here is including a nori sheet inside of the collard leaf, which helps to better bind the wrap, while adding tremendous savory flavor.*

8 large collard greens, without rips or holes

2 avocados

¾ cup Goji Salsa (page 155), or store-bought fresh salsa

4 raw nori sheets, cut in half

¼ teaspoon sea salt

several large handfuls of baby greens

large handful sprouts (such as mung bean, sunflower, or your favorite)

2 cups shredded carrots

1 batch Savory Seed Spread (page 158)

### SUPERFOOD TIP

For maximum nutrition, using collard greens raw is a win. Yet briefly blanching the leaves is a helpful option for a more pliable "wrapper." To blanch, simply dip each leaf in boiling water for 10 seconds, then immediately submerge in a bath of ice water. Dry before using.

To prepare the collards (after optional blanching—see the Superfood Tip below), lay one leaf at a time flat on a cutting board—lighter side facing up. Cut off the end stem, then carefully shave away the protruding center ridge of the stem with a knife, so the stem is fairly flush with the leaf. Repeat with remaining leaves and set aside.

In a medium bowl, mash the avocados with a fork. Mix in the Goji Salsa and add the sea salt. Keep covered until ready to use.

To assemble the wraps, take a leaf and lay it on a flat surface with the lighter side facing up and the spine vertical to you. Lay a nori strip horizontally across the leaf, about 2 inches up from the bottom (closest) end. Spread a couple spoonfuls of guacamole along the nori, leaving about an inch from each horizontal side. Place a few baby greens on top of the guacamole, followed by a layer of sprouts and carrots. Crumble some of the Savory Seed Spread on top. Pack the filling together a bit with your fingers, then curl the bottom leafy edge tightly over the filling. If the leaf is large enough, tuck the sides in, and roll up like a burrito. With the edge down to keep the wrap intact, cut on a diagonal in half to serve. Repeat with remaining wraps.

# STIR-FRIED BABY BOK CHOY WITH SHIITAKE MUSHROOMS, SUGAR SNAP PEAS & SACHA INCHI

MAKES 4 SERVINGS

*The trick to a good stir-fry is fresh ingredients, high heat, and extra-fast cooking for perfect "crisp-tender" vegetables. The kelp in this recipe adds extra minerals . . . and a little goes a long way. Additionally, the sacha inchi feels like it was born to be in this Asian-inspired combination and rounds out the nutrient-rich vegetables with healthy fats and protein.*

1 tablespoon miso paste

1 teaspoon powdered kelp

1 teaspoon yacon syrup

⅓ cup water

2 tablespoons coconut oil, divided

½ teaspoon sesame oil

3 cloves garlic, minced

2 cups shiitake mushroom caps, cut into ½-inch strips

2 cups sugar snap peas, trimmed

1 pound baby bok choy, sliced in half, lengthwise

¼ teaspoon red pepper flakes

1½ tablespoons ume plum vinegar

¼ cup sacha inchi seeds, chopped

cooked quinoa (page 138) or cooked brown rice, for serving

Briefly blend the miso, kelp, yacon syrup, and water in a small blender (or whisk together in a bowl until incorporated).

Heat both the coconut and sesame oils together in a large wok or skillet until you see a wisp of smoke. Over high heat, add the garlic, and stir-fry for about 30 seconds. Add the mushrooms and stir-fry for 1 minute. Add the sugar snap peas, bok choy, the miso blend, and red pepper flakes, and stir-fry until the bok choy is bright green and crisp-tender, about 5 minutes. Add the vinegar and cook for about 10 seconds. Transfer to a serving plate and top with sacha inchi seeds. Serve hot with cooked quinoa or rice.

## SUPERFOOD TIP

Despite common cooking lore, mushrooms can indeed be washed right before cooking and are not dependent on "dry brushing" as a sole cleaning method. Do note, however, that the stems of shiitake mushrooms are of a different makeup than other culinary varieties—shiitake stems are unpleasantly woody, and should be discarded.

# BLACK BEAN–HEMP PROTEIN PATTIES

## MAKES 6–8 PATTIES

*These patties are packed with premium protein, essential fatty acids, iron, calcium, fiber, and trace minerals, and won't contribute one bit to heart disease or diabetes, like animal-derived burgers do. Perfectly aligned spices celebrate three plant-based protein sources: black beans, hemp seeds, and quinoa.*

coconut oil, for cooking

1 cup finely diced sweet yellow onion (about ½ medium onion)

4 large cloves garlic, minced

1 cup finely diced red bell pepper (about 1 pepper)

1½ cups cooked black beans (unsalted)

1 cup hemp seeds

10 sun-dried tomatoes, soaked in hot water until soft, finely minced

½ teaspoon sea salt

2 teaspoons paprika powder

¼ teaspoon chipotle powder

¼ teaspoon cayenne powder

2 teaspoons miso paste

1 cup cooked brown rice

⅓ cup quinoa flakes

### SUPERFOOD TIP
Using unsalted beans in recipes allows maximum control over salt levels. If using salted beans, wait until the very end of the recipe to add any salt, then use to taste.

Heat 1 teaspoon coconut oil in a nonstick frying pan over medium heat. Add the onion and garlic, and cook until onion begins to turn translucent, about 3–4 minutes. Add the bell pepper, and continue to cook until vegetables have softened—about 5 minutes. Reduce the heat to low and add the black beans, hemp seeds, sun-dried tomatoes, sea salt, paprika, chipotle, and cayenne. Cook, stirring constantly, for an additional 1–2 minutes. Remove from heat and transfer to a large bowl.

Add the miso paste into the mixture. Use the back of a fork to mix the beans and miso together, partially mashing the beans. Mix in the cooked brown rice and quinoa flakes. When cool enough to handle, use clean hands to knead the mixture together to form a dense base. Place in the refrigerator, covered, for 30 minutes to allow quinoa flakes to swell and absorb the excess moisture.

Form the mixture into 6–8 patties, squeezing and packing the mixture together. (If necessary, a spoonful or two of water may be added to make the patties stick together easier.) Warm a small amount of coconut oil in a nonstick frying pan over medium heat. When the pan is hot, add the patties. Cook for about 4–5 minutes on each side, or until browned.

**Serving Suggestions:** Pair with spouted grain hamburger buns, avocado, tomatoes, onions, and sprouts. Or, try it "high protein-style"—tucked inside a collard leaf wrap or on top of a salad. Regardless of the serving method, including a smear of Maqui Ketchup (page 158) makes these delectable burgers absolutely outstanding.

# INCAN PATTIES

*Corn, quinoa, and sacha inchi (aka the Incan Peanut) were among the staple foods of the ancient Inca empire, whose people were known for their strength and resilience. In addition to these stamina-building foods, this recipe features Great Northern beans, which have the highest nutrient density of all beans.*

coconut oil, for cooking

1 shallot, minced (about ¼ cup)

3 cloves garlic, minced

½ celery stalk, minced

¼ cup cherry tomatoes, diced

1 teaspoon fresh thyme, minced

½ teaspoon fresh rosemary, minced

1 cup cooked Great Northern beans (or other white bean)

1 teaspoon Dijon mustard

¾ cup cooked brown rice

¼ cup quinoa flakes

½ cup sacha inchi seeds, finely chopped

¾ cup corn kernels, fresh or frozen (and thawed)

sea salt, if desired

Heat a small amount of coconut oil (about ½ tablespoon) over medium heat in a large nonstick skillet. Add the shallot, garlic, and celery, and sauté for a few minutes to soften. Mix in the cherry tomatoes, thyme, rosemary, and beans. Let the ingredients cook down for a few minutes to soften the tomatoes and release the flavors of the herbs, while at the same time using the back of a wooden spoon to both stir and mash down the beans and tomatoes.

After the ingredients are soft and incorporated, turn off the heat and transfer the contents of the pan to a medium bowl. Add the Dijon mustard, rice, quinoa flakes, sacha inchi, and corn. Mash everything together. Taste, adjusting the salt and seasonings if necessary, then cover and let stand for 15 minutes.

Using clean hands, form the mixture into 4 round patties, each about 1 inch thick. Heat a small amount of coconut oil in large nonstick skillet over medium heat, using just enough oil to cover the surface. Carefully place the patties inside the hot pan. Cook for about 10–12 minutes total, flipping the patties halfway through, until both sides form a golden crust.

**Serving Suggestion:** Try serving on top of a bed of arugula lightly dressed with Lemon-Camu Vinaigrette (page 96).

# QUINOA WITH SECRET PESTO & SUN-DRIED TOMATOES

## MAKES 4–6 SERVINGS

*A tasty pesto sauce with some very nutritious secrets, this recipe is a superfood twist on classic Italian dish.*

½ cup (packed) sun-dried tomatoes

✳ 2 cups (packed) chopped fresh basil

✳ ½ cup hemp seeds

⅓ cup EFA oil

⅓ cup olive oil

✳ 1 teaspoon freeze-dried wheatgrass powder

1 teaspoon nutritional yeast

¾ teaspoon sea salt

1 tablespoon minced garlic

✳ 4 cups cooked quinoa

✳ 2 cups (packed) baby spinach, cut chiffonade-style (a.k.a. extra thin)

Soak the sun-dried tomatoes in hot water for 30 minutes or until soft. Slice thinly.

Use a food processor to blend the basil, hemp seeds, both oils, wheatgrass powder, nutritional yeast, sea salt, and garlic into a pesto sauce. In a large bowl, toss some of the pesto (use as much as desired) with the quinoa, sun-dried tomatoes, and spinach. Serve cold, or gently heat.

## BASIC QUINOA COOKING METHOD

1 part dry quinoa : scant 2 parts water
1 cup dry quinoa = 3 cups cooked quinoa

Rinse the quinoa (some quinoa is sold pre-rinsed) using a fine mesh sieve or strainer. Combine the quinoa and water in a pot and bring to a boil, then reduce heat to a simmer. Cook for about 15 minutes, or until the water has evaporated and the quinoa is slightly translucent and tender. Let stand for 5 minutes and fluff with a fork before serving.

# TOFU-BROCCOLI QUICHE
# WITH QUINOA CRUST

MAKES ONE 9-INCH QUICHE

*I've never been much of a fan of either sweet or savory pastry. That's why I like this quiche. Aside from using tofu for the filling (which makes exceptional quiches that are light and springy, as well as free of the cholesterol found in eggs), the "crust" is made from toothsome quinoa. Though it's not pastry-like in any way, it's delicious nonetheless. Bonus: This quiche is even better the next day.*

## FOR THE CRUST

- ⅓ cup flaxseed powder
- ⅓ cup warm water
- 2 cups cooked quinoa (page 138)
- 3 tablespoons melted coconut oil, plus extra for baking pan
- ¼ cup nutritional yeast
- ¼ teaspoon sea salt

## FOR THE FILLING

- 1 tablespoon coconut oil
- 1 cup finely chopped yellow onion
- 4 large cloves garlic, minced
- 2 cups finely chopped broccoli florets (chopped to dice-size or smaller)
- 1 pound (16 ounces) firm tofu
- ¼ cup nutritional yeast
- 2 tablespoons tahini
- 1 tablespoon ume plum vinegar
- ½ teaspoon ground tumeric

Mix the flaxseed powder and water together in a small bowl and set aside for ten minutes to "gel." Preheat the oven to 400° F. Lightly grease the bottom and sides of a 9-inch pie pan with coconut oil.

In a large bowl, mix together the quinoa, coconut oil, nutritional yeast, and sea salt. Add in the flaxseed gel and stir well. Spread the mixture evenly onto the bottom of the prepared pie pan. Use your hands to firmly pack the unbaked crust into a dense, flat, compact layer. Pre-bake for 10 minutes and remove from oven until ready for use.

For the filling, melt 1 tablespoon of coconut oil in a nonstick pan over medium heat. Add the onion and garlic, and sauté for 2 minutes until softened. Add the broccoli, and cook for 3 minutes longer, until broccoli begins to turn bright green. Remove from heat and set aside.

In a food processor or blender, whip the tofu, nutritional yeast, tahini, ume vinegar, and tumeric together until smooth. Add the cooked vegetables and utilize the pulse function 3 or 4 times to incorporate the vegetables but not blend. Use a spatula or spoon to transfer the mixture into the prepared quinoa pie crust. Bake for 45–50 minutes, or until top is golden brown. Remove from heat and let stand for 10 minutes before serving; quiche is delicious served either hot or cold.

# TERIYAKI SHIITAKE SUSHI

### MAKES 4 SERVINGS

*Sushi gets an instant and fun makeover by using quinoa in place of sushi rice, with a little hit of flaxseed powder mixed in to keep it "sticky." An outrageously good Superfood Teriyaki Sauce (boosted with maca) makes the marinated shiitake mushrooms inside the rolls tender and burst with flavor.*

¾ cup shiitake mushroom caps, sliced

1 batch Superfood Teriyaki Sauce

1 cup uncooked quinoa

2 cups water

2 tablespoons flaxseed powder

2 teaspoons yacon syrup

1 teaspoon of miso paste

4 nori sheets

1 avocado, peeled, pitted, and thinly sliced

½ cup sunflower sprouts, pea shoots, or microgreens

Place the mushrooms in a small bowl and pour the Superfood Teriyaki Sauce on top. Mix well. Cover and refrigerate for 30 minutes.

Meanwhile, combine the quinoa and water in a saucepan, bring to a boil, then reduce heat to a simmer. Cook uncovered for 15 minutes, or until quinoa is soft and water has evaporated. Remove from heat and immediately add the flaxseed powder, yacon syrup, and miso. Mix well, and cool to room temperature.

Use a fork to remove the mushrooms, squeezing out any extra moisture, and set aside. Reserve the remaining teriyaki marinade for a dipping sauce. Roll the ingredients into sushi (see page 143) or hand rolls, using the quinoa as the "rice," and the mushrooms, avocado, and sprouts as the filling.

### SUPERFOOD TERIYAKI SAUCE

3 tablespoons yacon syrup

3 tablespoons shoyu (or soy sauce)

1 tablespoon EFA oil

1 tablespoon orange juice

2 tablespoons water

¼ teaspoon onion powder

¼ teaspoon garlic powder

1 tablespoon freshly grated ginger root

1 tablespoon maca powder

2 tablespoons sesame seeds (raw or toasted)

Combine all the ingredients in a small bowl and whisk together. Will keep for about 2 weeks, refrigerated. Makes ⅔ cup.

# ARUGULA & TEMPEH SUSHI

*Add a little extra protein to your next veggie roll with this creative sushi. Though any type of tempeh can be used, a wild rice tempeh works particularly well.*

8 ounces tempeh, finely crumbled

2 tablespoons coconut oil

2 tablespoons miso paste

2 tablespoons tahini

2 teaspoons fresh lemon juice

4 cups (packed) chopped arugula

20 sun-dried tomatoes, soaked in hot water for 30 minutes to soften, then thinly sliced

½ cup Quick Pickled Onions (page 104)

4–6 nori sheets

Stir-fry the tempeh in the coconut oil for 3–4 minutes over medium heat, or until tempeh turns golden brown. Remove from heat and mix with the miso, tahini, and lemon juice. Let cool to room temperature.

Roll the ingredients into sushi (see steps below) using the tempeh in the place of rice, and the arugula, tomatoes, and onions as the filling. Slice each roll into 6–8 pieces, and serve. (Alternatively, form into hand rolls.)

## 5 STEPS TO HOMEMADE SUSHI ROLLS

Homemade sushi takes a little practice, but is likely easier than you think.

ONE: Place the nori shiny side down, on a bamboo mat, with the line indents vertical to you.

TWO: Spread a handful of rice (or rice substitute) horizontally across the bottom half of the sheet. Pat down the rice to make it even.

THREE: Lay the filling ingredients in a horizontal line across the center of the rice.

FOUR: Beginning on the side closest to you, roll the sushi up like a jelly roll while using the mat to tuck, squeeze, and compact, forming a tight cylinder. Moisten the nori edge with water, and hold for a moment to seal.

FIVE: Dip a sharp knife into hot water before cutting, then gently saw the sushi into rounds.

# GARDEN LASAGNA

## MAKES 8–10 SERVINGS

*Admittedly, this recipe may not win the quick award, but the results are oh-so-rewarding (EFAs, protein, fiber, calcium, iron), not to mention delicious. This noodle-free recipe (hello, eggplant rounds!) is a bit like a casserole- lasagna fusion; for a more traditional lasagna, buckwheat lasagna noodles can be added to the layers.*

2 large eggplants

olive oil, for broiling

sea salt

4 cups (packed) fresh spinach and/or kale, chopped

Tomato Sauce
Lentil-Hemp Filling
Sunflower Spread

Prepare the Tomato Sauce, Lentil-Hemp Filling, and Sunflower Spread first, as directed on the opposite page.

Set the oven to broil. Line three baking sheets with aluminum foil and brush foil with a little olive oil. Peel the eggplant and cut off the ends, then slice into ¼-inch slices. Line the baking sheets with the eggplant and brush the rounds with a little olive oil on both sides, and dust lightly with sea salt. Broil for 8–10 minutes, flipping halfway through, until golden and soft. Remove from heat.

Lower the oven temperature to 350° F. Line the bottom of a 4-quart lasagna pan with a flat layer of the eggplant rounds. Spread a third of the Tomato Sauce on top. Crumble half of the Lentil-Hemp Filling over the sauce, then layer half of the spinach on top of the filling. Distribute the Sunflower Spread over the spinach/kale in small dollops. Repeat the layers, with the top/last layer being the remaining tomato sauce. Spread out gently to smooth and flatten the surface of the lasagna. Cover with aluminum foil, and bake for 30 minutes, or until heated through. Serve warm.

## TOMATO SAUCE

2 cups sun-dried tomatoes (unsalted)

4 cups very warm water

1 tablespoon coconut oil

2 cups chopped yellow onion (about 1 onion)

6 large cloves garlic, minced

4 cups chopped tomatoes

1/3 cup red wine

1/4 cup basil, minced

sea salt, to taste

Steep the sun-dried tomatoes in the warm water and set aside to soak for 20 minutes to soften. Meanwhile, melt the coconut oil in a large pan over medium-high heat. Add the onions and cook, 3–4 minutes, until the onion begins to turn translucent, then add the garlic and cook for a minute longer. Add the chopped tomatoes to the pan, along with the red wine, and cook for 5 minutes, or until tomatoes are soft. Stir in the basil, and remove from heat. Transfer the vegetables to a food processor along with the soaked sun-dried tomatoes and 1 cup of the soak water (reserve remaining 1 cup soak water for the Sunflower Spread below). Blend into a chunky sauce. Check flavor and add salt if desired.

## LENTIL- HEMP FILLING

2 1/2 cups cooked lentils

1 1/2 tablespoons miso paste

2 tablespoons tahini

2 tablespoons fresh minced oregano

2 tablespoons fresh minced basil

2 tablespoons fresh squeezed lemon juice

1 teaspoon garlic powder

1/3 cup hemp seeds

1/2 tablespoon coconut oil

In a medium bowl, mix together all the filling ingredients (except the oil) until combined. Heat the oil in a frying pan, then add the prepared mixture. Cook over low heat for 2–3 minutes, stirring constantly, then set aside to cool.

## SUNFLOWER SPREAD

1 cup sunflower seeds

1/2 cup cashews

1 1/2 tablespoons miso

1 tablespoon nutritional yeast

3/4 cup sun-dried tomato soak water (from tomato sauce, above) plus 1/4 cup on hand, if needed

Blend the ingredients together into a ricotta-like paste. Depending on the blender, this may require stopping the machine a few times and scraping down the sides before blending again. Use the reserved 1/4 cup soak water only if needed—the finished mixture should be very thick.

# SIDES

*You can't help but feel a bit of pride chowing down on an irresistible side dish while knowing that it's secretly packed with superfoods. Maca on sweet potato fries? Tater-like tots nutritious enough to eat as a whole meal? You bet. Just because these are small bites doesn't mean they can't offer huge benefits.*

# BBQ SWEET POTATO FRIES

*Coconut oil and sweet potatoes are a match made in foodie heaven. Add this special homemade spice blend that sneaks in a little maca powder, and expect the general consensus to be nothing short of "wow."*

2 pounds sweet potatoes

2 tablespoons coconut oil, melted

1¼ teaspoons paprika

½ teaspoon chili powder

¼ teaspoon garlic powder

¾ teaspoon onion powder

1 teaspoon mesquite powder

½ teaspoon maca powder

⅛ teaspoon cayenne pepper

¾ teaspoon sea salt

1 teaspoon coconut sugar

### SUPERFOOD TIP

The peel on root vegetables is where the most nutrition is, and sweet potatoes are no exception. Roasting these fries unpeeled locks in more flavor and offers extra minerals.

Preheat the oven to 450° F.

Cut the sweet potatoes into long fries, about ½-inch thick. Toss with melted coconut oil and spread out flat onto 2 baking sheets. Place in the oven and roast for about 15–25 minutes, until fries are cooked through and begin to brown. (Cook for an additional 5–10 minutes for crispier fries.)

While the fries are cooking, mix together all the spice powders and remaining dry ingredients in a small bowl.

When the fries have finished roasting, remove the pans from the oven and immediately sprinkle some of the spice mixture on top (use amount to taste), tossing the fries around with a spatula to ensure even coating. Serve warm with Maqui Ketchup (page 158) or regular ketchup, if desired.

# TATER (-LIKE) TOTS

MAKES 4–6 SERVINGS

*Crispy on the outside and perfectly soft on the inside, these tater-like tots really do wonders for comfort cravings. Yet this recipe has a BIG secret—instead of using potatoes, these tots are actually made entirely from highly nutritious foods. With loads of protein, EFAs, and fiber—and made without a deep fryer—these are by far the most delicious and nutritious tots around.*

1 ½ cups cooked Great Northern beans (or other white bean)

✂ ¼ cup flaxseed powder

✂ ¼ cup golden flaxseeds

✂ 2 cups cooked quinoa (page 138)

2 tablespoons mild white miso

¼ cup brown rice flour

½ cup onion, finely minced

coconut oil, for cooking

Using a fork, mash the beans* in a large bowl. Mix in all the remaining ingredients, except for oil.

Using a handful of dough at a time, form long logs, about 1-inch thick, on a chopping board. Carefully cut the logs into ½-inch slices to make the tots.

Warm a nonstick pan over low heat and add a little coconut oil to coat the pan. Place tots inside the pan and cook for several minutes, until golden brown underneath. Use a spatula to flip the tots over to brown the other sides evenly.

Serve immediately, with Maqui Ketchup (page 158) or regular ketchup, if desired.

*Unless you're making them fresh (bonus points for you!), canned Great Northern beans are generally sold pre-salted. If unsalted beans are in fact used/available, extra miso may be added to taste to increase the flavor.

# ROASTED PARSNIP PUREE WITH MAPLE SACHA INCHI

### MAKES 4 SERVINGS

*Smooth, creamy, and oh-so-flavorful parsnips take the place of tired mashed potatoes in this exceptional side dish. Although sophisticated in flavor, the recipe is actually quite simple . . . the most difficult part is garnering the willpower to avoid eating all of the freshly roasted parsnips straight out of the oven (hint: make extra). I'm also a little obsessed with the maple sacha inchi here, which adds just the right bit of sweetness and crunch.*

2 pounds parsnips, peeled and cut into ½-inch chunks

2 tablespoons coconut oil, melted
sea salt, to taste

⅓ cup sacha inchi seeds

1 tablespoon maple syrup

1¼ cups water

Preheat the oven to 400° F.

On a large baking tray, toss the parsnips with the melted coconut oil, and sprinkle with a little sea salt. Bake for about 25–30 minutes, tossing once to flip, until parsnips are golden brown. Remove from the oven and keep warm until ready to make the puree.

While the parsnips are cooking, tear off a square of parchment paper and place on top of a plate. In a small pan, heat the sacha inchi seeds over medium-low heat for 3–4 minutes, tossing frequently so as not to burn. Add a pinch of sea salt, then pour in the maple syrup and immediately turn off the heat. Stir the seeds well to coat them in the sizzling syrup. After about a minute of stirring, transfer the pan contents to the prepared plate and spread out to cool and dry.

Transfer the roasted parsnips to a food processor and puree. Slowly add the water while the machine is running, a little at a time, until the puree has reached the desired consistency. Season with sea salt to taste. Transfer the mixture to a serving bowl, and top with the sacha inchi to serve.

# TOMATILLO CHIA SALSA

## MAKES ABOUT 2 CUPS

*The longer this salsa sits, the better—it is even more flavorful the next day. If you don't like cilantro, it can be omitted, or, if you do, more can be added for extra flavor. Chia seeds help keep this tangy salsa light and bright.*

- 2 tablespoons chia seeds
- 1 medium cucumber, diced
- ¾ pound fresh tomatillos (husks removed), diced
- ½ tablespoon fresh lime juice
- 2 – 3 tablespoons fresh cilantro leaves
- ¼ cup white onion, diced
- 2 cloves garlic, minced
- 1 jalapeño pepper, de-seeded and minced
- ¼ teaspoon sea salt

Use a food processor to pulse all the ingredients together into a chunky salsa—do not blend or salsa will become a soup. (You can also simply chop and mix the ingredients by hand.) Refrigerate for a minimum of 30 minutes before serving to allow the flavors to develop and the chia seeds to absorb some of the excess liquid. Use with your favorite chips or crackers, or tuck inside of a wrap or burrito as a flavorful spread.

**Variation:** Mix 1 (peeled and pitted) chopped avocado into the finished salsa.

# GOJI SALSA

## MAKES ABOUT 1 ½ CUPS

*It makes sense that goji berries go so well with tomatoes: They are both members of the nightshade family of plants, making them kind of distant cousins. You'll find that goji's mild sweetness acts almost like a perfectly ripe cherry tomato in this beautiful, fresh, and easy-to-prepare salsa.*

- ½ cup dried goji berries
- 1 cup tomatoes, diced
- 1 clove garlic, minced
- ½ medium shallot, minced
- ½ jalapeño pepper, de-seeded and minced
- 1 tablespoon fresh lime juice

Toss all ingredients together in a medium bowl. Refrigerate for a minimum of 30 minutes before serving to allow the goji berries to plump up and the flavors to marry. Use with your favorite chips or crackers, or tuck inside of a wrap or burrito as a flavorful spread.

# OLIVE CAVIAR

### MAKES ⅔ CUP

*This bold, briny, tapanade-inspired dip is excellent on crackers and vegetables, or used as a spread in sandwiches or wraps. It can also be enjoyed as a beautiful pasta sauce.*

1 cup pitted kalamata olives

2 tablespoons dulse flakes

1 tablespoon chia seeds

¼ cup water

½ teaspoon Dijon mustard

1 large clove garlic, minced

1 teaspoon fresh lemon juice

1 tablespoon EFA oil

Place all ingredients in a food processor, and puree. Let the dip stand for at least 15 minutes to allow the chia seeds to bulk up and the flavors to develop. Will keep for several weeks, refrigerated.

# HEMP HUMMUS

### MAKES ABOUT 2 CUPS

*This creamy dip goes especially well with crackers and raw vegetables, or used as a spread in sandwiches or wraps. The addition of hemp seeds provides a superb boost of protein, essential fatty acids, iron, and chlorophyll.*

1½ cups garbanzo beans (freshly sprouted or cooked unsalted)

2 tablespoons tahini

¼ cup hemp seeds

1 tablespoon EFA oil

1½ teaspoons garlic powder

⅓ cup fresh lemon juice

¾ teaspoon sea salt

½ teaspoon smoked paprika (optional)

In a food processor, blend all ingredients until smooth and creamy. Transfer to a bowl and serve. Will keep for 1 week, refrigerated.

# SAVORY SEED SPREAD

## MAKES ABOUT 1 CUP

*When no one is looking, I like to take this spread and roll it up inside a nori sheet like a thin cigar for an awesome snack. However, if strange-looking foods aren't up your ally, try it as a filling for a wrap or sandwich, or lodged into celery slices as a quick bite. It's packed with protein, beautifying fats, and minerals.*

- ⅔ cup hemp seeds
- 2 tablespoons flaxseed powder
- ¼ cup raw sunflower seeds
- 2 tablespoons lemon juice
- 1 tablespoon miso paste
- 1 tablespoon nutritional yeast
- ¼ teaspoon dried oregano
- ¼ teaspoon garlic powder
- ¼ teaspoon onion powder

Mix all the ingredients together in a bowl until combined. Will keep for about 1 week, refrigerated.

# MAQUI KETCHUP

## MAKES ABOUT 1 CUP

*Even the most unassuming of condiments can be the perfect place to pack in antioxidants and natural energy.*

- 1 tablespoon maqui powder
- 4 tablespoons tomato paste
- 3 tablespoons apple cider vinegar
- 1 tablespoon ume plum vinegar
- 1 teaspoon onion powder
- 1 tablespoon agave nectar
- 1 Medjool date, pit removed

Blend all the ingredients together in small (single-serving) blender until combined. Will keep for about 1 week, refrigerated.

# INCAN BERRY–CRANBERRY CHUTNEY

*Inspired by traditional cranberry sauce recipes, this sweet and tart chutney is filled with classic Incan power foods like chia seeds and goldenberries, which are a superb match for cranberry's unique flavor. Whether used as a sauce, served as a side dish (great for holidays), or eaten straight out of the bowl, this antioxidant-rich and flavorful mixture is absolutely heavenly.*

- ¼ cup chia seeds
- 1 cup unsweetened cranberry juice
- 3 tablespoons yacon syrup
- ⅓ cup + ¼ cup dried goldenberries (divided)
- ½ cup soft Medjool dates (about 5 or 6), pits removed

Mix together the chia seeds, cranberry juice, yacon syrup, and ⅓ cup of goldenberries. Refrigerate for a minimum of an hour (up to overnight) to let goldenberries soften and the chia seeds plump up.

When the goldenberries are soft, place the mixture into a food processor, and add the dates. Process until chunky. Stop the machine, add the remaining ¼ cup of goldenberries, and pulse a few times to coarsely chop the berries while leaving some texture. Best served chilled.

# SWEET SAGE CREAM

MAKES ABOUT 1 ½ CUPS

*A special condiment that begs to adorn warm cooked winter squashes and roasted vegetables. Lasts for 1 week.*

- ½ cup dried yacon slices
- 1¼ cups hot water
- 1 cup raw cashews
- ½ teaspoon sea salt
- 2 tablespoons coconut oil
- ⅔ cup shallots, minced
- ¼ cup fresh sage leaves, minced

Soak the yacon slices in the hot water for 10 minutes. Once a tea has formed, discard the slices (or enjoy as a snack!) and pour the tea into a small blender with the cashews and salt. Blend into a smooth cream.

Heat the coconut oil in a pan over medium heat, and add the shallots and sage. Cook for 2 minutes, stirring constantly. Add this mixture to the blender with the cream, and process again until smooth. Pour everything back into the pan, and cook over low heat, stirring, for 2 minutes.

# BUTTERY SPREAD

MAKES 2 CUPS

*Granted, there are no bona fide superfoods in this recipe, but if butter were ever to have benefits, this is the closest it would come. This creamy spread serves as an all-natural, plant-based, cholesterol-free replacement for butter and margarine. Whether you're intolerant of diary, avoiding unhealthy trans-fats, or just looking for another way to promote a high energy and a lean physique (thanks coconut oil!)—this spread works like magic. It even melts!*

2 cups raw cashews

1 cup coconut oil, melted

¼ teaspoon sea salt

In a high-speed blender or food processor, blend all ingredients together until completely smooth (this will take a minute or two, depending on your machine; be patient). Pour into a 16-ounce glass jar with lid, and refrigerate to solidify. When stored in the refrigerator, Buttery Spread keeps 2 months.

# GARLIC BUTTERY SPREAD

MAKES 2 CUPS

*A small variation on Buttery Spread, this recipe is so close to real garlic butter, it may just have your audience fooled. Use it to enhance savory recipes, smear on crackers and breads, or melt on top of warm quinoa, rice, or steamed vegetables.*

2 cups raw cashews

1 cup coconut oil, melted

¼ teaspoon sea salt

1 teaspoon garlic powder

In a high-speed blender or food processor, blend all ingredients together until completely smooth (this will take a minute or two, depending on your machine; be patient). Pour into a 16-ounce glass jar with lid, and refrigerate to solidify. When stored in the refrigerator, Garlic Buttery Spread keeps 2 months.

# SNACKS

It's no secret that humans were designed to eat in a grazing fashion. Instead of sitting down for a few large meals and eating until full, snacking lightly throughout the day helps maintain consistent energy and, surprisingly, helps control the appetite. Of course, the source of the snacks makes all the difference! These natural snacks serve as an excellent way to quell hunger, stave off cravings, and provide energy. Super-seeds like flax and chia do wonders here, often taking the place of empty-calorie flours. Stock your kitchen with these grab-able goodies and experience the difference of superfood snacking.

# ENERGIZER TRAIL MIX

## MAKES ABOUT 6 CUPS

*You've never had a trail mix quite like this one! Phenomenal for keeping your energy up with well-rounded nutrients, this snack is filled with all the lively flavors and textures of top-notch superfoods, making it a true pleasure to eat. It lasts for literally months, and couldn't be simpler to make! Try to find large coconut flakes as opposed to shredded coconut—the flakes are easier to snack on.*

1 cup dried goji berries

1 cup dried mulberries

½ cup raisins

1 cup sacha inchi seeds

1 cup unsweetened coconut flakes

¾ cup raw pecans

⅓ cup cacao nibs

Toss all the ingredients together in a bowl, and store in an airtight container. Will keep for several months.

### SUPERFOOD TIP

Trail mixes reach back to the way our ancient ancestors ate—grazing throughout the day on a collection of food that made them feel good and would last a long time throughout their nomadic travels. Although the flavors in this mix balance each other very well, feel free to experiment with other favorite superfoods like dried goldenberries, dried blueberries, or even superfood granola (such as Banana-Hemp Granola, page 64).

# LAND & SEA TRAIL MIX

## MAKES ABOUT 6 CUPS

*This special recipe was born out of the desire for a trail mix that wasn't sweet, but rather savory, salty, crispy, crunchy, satisfying, and altogether munch-worthy . . . while still being healthy. This mix meets those demands and then some—using vegetables from both the land and the sea to produce a very high-mineral snack. Ideal for a hike, camping trip, or just as a midday power chow.*

- 1 bunch green kale, stems discarded, leaves torn into large pieces
- 6 raw nori sheets
- 1 tablespoon minced shallot
- ½ teaspoon garlic powder
- 2 tablespoons yacon syrup
- 2 tablespoons shoyu
- 1 tablespoon apple cider vinegar
- 2 teaspoons sesame oil
- ½ teaspoon ginger powder
- ¼ cup raw sesame seeds
- ½ cup raw sunflower seeds
- ¾ cup raw walnuts, coarsely chopped

---

### SUPERFOOD TIP

When dehydrating (or lightly baking) delicate vegetables like kale, always be sure to dry the leaves as thoroughly as possible after washing to cut down on cooking time.

---

Place the kale leaves inside a large bowl and crumble the nori on top. Toss well. Add in all the remaining ingredients, and use clean hands to massage together for 1–2 minutes. Proceed with your method of choice below.

**Dehydrator Method (preferred):** Spread the mixture evenly atop 3 or 4 mesh dehydrator sheets. Dehydrate at 115° F or desired temperature* until kale is crispy and dried through (about 6–12 hours).

**Oven Method:** Heat the oven to 200° F. Line a baking sheet with parchment paper, and distribute the mixture evenly across the surface. Place the tray in the oven and cook for 80–95 minutes, or until kale is dried out and crispy. For best results and fastest cooking, toss the mixture once or twice during the second half of cooking time, and check frequently towards the end of cooking to ensure the vegetables do not burn. Let cool completely on the tray before serving.

Store in an airtight container when not in use to help prevent the kale from becoming soft. Will keep for about 1–2 weeks.

*Dehydrators don't burn food, so you can dehydrate at as low a temperature as you wish (for maximum nutritional content), or use a higher temperature (for a faster turnaround time).

# CHEESY KALE CRISPS

## MAKES 2–4 SERVINGS

*If you've never had kale crisps before, you're in for a real treat. (And if you have, get ready for one of the best recipes around—seriously.) These have a distinctly Parmesan-like flavor that is excitingly addicting. Just watch: even people who "don't like kale" will transform into kale-munching monsters before your very eyes (kids included). Better just go ahead and start a second batch now.*

- 1 large bunch of curly green kale
- 2 tablespoons coconut oil, melted
- 2 tablespoons flaxseed powder
- 1 teaspoon fresh lemon juice
- 1 tablespoon nutritional yeast
- 1 tablespoon tahini
- 1 teaspoon onion powder
- ¼ teaspoon sea salt, or to taste

### SUPERFOOD TIP

Although they rarely last due to addictive healthy munching, kale crisps often lose some of their crunch rather quickly, even when stored inside air-tight containers. For an easy (and free!) way to "keep the crisp," save the small silica packets found in packages of seaweed and other snacks, and reuse them by placing inside your container of kale crisps. Very effective!

Wash the kale and dry very thoroughly (otherwise the flavorings will not coat the leaves well). Remove the thick parts of the stem from the kale leaves, and tear the leaves into large pieces in a big bowl.

In a small bowl or cup, mix together the oil, flaxseed powder, lemon juice, nutritional yeast, tahini, onion powder, and sea salt. Pour this mixture into the kale bowl.

Using clean hands, massage the oil mixture into the kale, squeezing and tossing the vegetables as you go to help soften the leaves. Mix for about 2 minutes until leaves are evenly coated. Taste and adjust salt if needed. Proceed with your method of choice below.

**Dehydrator Method (preferred):** Warm the dehydrator to 115° F. Spread out the kale onto 4 perforated dehydrator sheets, and dehydrate for 10–12 hours, or until crispy (time may vary depending on local humidity). When done, store in an air-tight, sealed container.

**Oven Method:** Heat the oven to 200° F. Spread the kale out as flatly as possible onto a couple of baking sheets lined with parchment paper. Bake for 55–80 minutes, or until kale has dried out and is crispy. Keep a close eye on the kale at the end of its cooking process to make sure it does not burn. Let cool, and store in an air-tight, sealed container.

# BUCKWHEAT GRAHAM CRACKERS

## MAKES ABOUT 5 DOZEN 2-INCH CRACKERS

*There's something so friendly about graham crackers, and this version is especially amiable with its protein (thanks, buckwheat flour and mesquite powder!), good fats, and important minerals like calcium. To make this regenerating snack extra crispy, add a few minutes to the cooking time.*

2 cups buckwheat flour

¼ cup mesquite powder, plus extra for rolling

¼ cup flaxseed powder

1 teaspoon baking soda

1 teaspoon sea salt

½ cup coconut sugar

⅓ cup unsweetened almond milk

¼ cup grade B maple syrup

¼ cup coconut oil, melted

2 tablespoons vanilla extract

In a food processor (or by hand), mix all the dry ingredients together, including the coconut sugar, until combined. Add in the remaining wet ingredients one by one, and process until a dough has formed; the dough should be firm and slightly sticky. If the dough is too dry, add additional almond milk, one teaspoon at a time. If dough is too wet, increase the buckwheat flour slightly. Divide the dough into two balls, cover, and refrigerate for 1 hour.

Preheat the oven to 325° F. Place a large piece of lightly floured parchment paper (use additional mesquite powder to flour it) on a flat countertop. Set one dough ball on top, and press down firmly to partially flatten. Place a second piece of floured parchment paper on top, and use a rolling pin to roll the dough into a very thin layer— about ⅛-inch thick. Place onto a baking sheet, and carefully remove top layer of parchment. Repeat with the other dough half, and place on a second baking sheet. With a pizza cutter or ravioli roller (or simply a knife), gently cut the dough into 2-inch squares. Use a fork to score each of the crackers with decorative dots. Bake crackers for 22–28 minutes or until dry, keeping a close watch at the end of cooking time so as not to burn.

Once removed from the oven, leave the crackers on the pan for 5 minutes, then transfer to a wire rack to finish cooling and become crisper. Kept in an airtight container, graham crackers will keep for about 2 weeks.

# GOOD SEED CRACKERS

## MAKES ABOUT 2 ½ DOZEN CRACKERS

*The good seeds—chia, hemp, and flax—combine forces in these delicious crackers, turning a simple snack into a nutritious feast. These seedy bites are packed with nutrition in every crunch—rich in protein, healthy fats, and fiber. They can also be crumbled to make a fantastic salad crouton.*

- ¼ cup chia seeds
- 2 tablespoons flaxseeds
- 6 tablespoons flaxseed powder
- 1 cup warm water
- ⅔ cup hemp seeds
- 2 tablespoons coconut oil, melted
- ½ teaspoon garlic powder
- ¾ teaspoon sea salt
- ¼ teaspoon black pepper

Place chia seeds, flaxseeds, and flaxseed powder into a bowl. Stir in the water, and let stand for 10 minutes to allow the seeds to hydrate. Once the mixture has thickened, stir in the hemp seeds, oil, garlic powder, salt, and pepper. Proceed with your method of choice below.

**Dehydrator method (preferred):** Spread the mixture out in a thin layer on a nonstick dehydrator sheet. With a knife, score the spread into squares for easy separation when dry. Dehydrate at 115° F or desired temperature* until crispy, flipping once for uniform dehydration (about 12–16 hours). Store in an airtight container.

**Oven method:** Spread the mixture onto parchment paper, forming an approximate 12 x 10-inch rectangle, smoothing out as evenly as possible. Bake at 250° F for 1 hour. After an hour, flip the crackers over and bake for 15 minutes longer, or until thinner areas have just begun to turn golden brown. Turn off the oven and let the crackers remain inside until the oven is cool, about 30 minutes. Break into pieces and store in an airtight container.

*Dehydrators don't burn food, so you can dehydrate at as low a temperature as you wish (for maximum nutritional content), or use a higher temperature (for a faster turnaround time).

# ROSEMARY ALMOND CRACKERS

## MAKES ABOUT 8 CUPS OF CRACKERS

*Despite their savory sophistication, these crackers were actually one of the very first recipes I made back when I was in college. I really wanted a food dehydrator, and so I did what any college kid would do: I asked my parents to buy me one. One birthday gift later, I soon fell into what I now consider my "year of dehydrated superfood crackers." These days, though I still love my dehydrator (same one!), I sometimes use an oven for this recipe when I want a faster turnaround time.*

½ cup golden flaxseeds

½ cup flaxseed powder

2 cups water

1 cup raw almonds, chopped

2 stalks celery, chopped

2 cloves garlic, minced

1 teaspoon sea salt

3 tablespoons fresh lemon juice

2 heaping tablespoons fresh rosemary, finely minced

Soak the whole flaxseeds and flaxseed powder in 2 cups water for 20 minutes, letting the seeds saturate and form a thick gel. Use a food processor to puree the flax mixture with all of the remaining ingredients, forming a dough. Proceed with your method of choice below.

**Dehydrator method (preferred):** With the back of a spatula, spread mixture thinly onto several nonstick dehydrator sheets. Dehydrate at 115° F or desired temperature* until mostly dry. Peel the mixture away from the sheet and cut into desired cracker shape. Continue dehydrating until crispy (about 10–14 hours total).

**Oven method:** Grease 2 baking sheets with coconut oil and spread mixture thinly on top. Bake at 300° F for 45–50 minutes, or until crackers just begin to turn golden brown—be careful not to burn. Cool slightly and break into pieces.

*Dehydrators don't burn food, so you can dehydrate at as low a temperature as you wish (for maximum nutritional content), or use a higher temperature (for a faster turnaround time).

# SESAME FLATBREAD

### MAKES 6 SERVINGS

*Before the invention of refined flours and "white" foods, ancient cultures made flatbreads: nutrient-rich crispy breads made from legumes, seeds, and whole grains. This version, which is high in protein, essential fatty acids, and important minerals like calcium, is a truly regenerating snack. It's amazing with a smear of Hemp Hummus (page 156), Olive Caviar (also page 156), or any of the other condiments in this book! To make the flatbread extra crispy, you can add a couple minutes to the cooking time.*

1 tablespoon coconut oil

2 tablespoons flaxseed powder

1 tablespoon chia seed powder

1½ cups cooked unsalted garbanzo beans

⅓ cup raw sesame seeds

1 tablespoon fresh lemon juice

2 tablespoon minced scallions (white and green parts)

½ teaspoon sea salt

Preheat the oven to 350° F. Line a baking sheet with parchment paper.

Place all ingredients in a food processor and blend to create a smooth dough. (Alternatively, mash the garbanzo beans into a smooth paste with a fork and mix/knead by hand.)

Form the dough into a ball, and use a rolling pin to flatten into a thin oval directly on the prepared baking sheet. (Roll gently to ensure that the dough does not stick to the rolling pin.) Once flattened into a ¼-inch layer, use your palms to continue to coax the dough to cover as much of the area of the baking sheet as possible in an even layer. Bake until just golden brown, about 30–40 minutes. Let the flatbread cool for 10 minutes, then remove from the baking tray and break apart, or cut into pieces.

For storage, keep in an airtight container for up to 1 week.

### SUPERFOOD TIP
Flaxseed powder and chia seed powder function very similarly in recipes when used in small amounts. Feel free to substitute one for the other, depending on what you have on hand.

# CHOCOLATE HEMP & OAT BARS

*An easy, healthy, granola-like bar that eats like a cookie. The cacao nibs, folded
in with sweet oats and nutty hemp seeds, give these bars a unique crunch.*

¼ cup + 1 teaspoon coconut oil

1 cup (packed) soft Medjool dates
(about 10 or 11 dates), pits removed

✖ ¼ cup hemp milk (page 224), or
store-bought nut milk of choice

1 tablespoon vanilla extract

✖ 1 tablespoon chia seed powder

1½ cups rolled oats*

½ cup wheat flour*

¾ teaspoon baking soda

½ teaspoon salt

✖ ⅓ cup hemp seeds

⅓ cup dark chocolate, finely chopped

✖ ¼ cup cacao nibs

*For gluten-free bars, use gluten-free
oats and flour, available through
natural food stores or online (see
Ingredient Resources Guide on
page 228).

Preheat oven to 350° F. Lightly grease a baking sheet with 1 teaspoon
of coconut oil.

In a small saucepan, melt the remaining coconut oil into a warm
liquid. Pour the coconut oil into a food processor, and add the dates,
hemp milk, vanilla extract, and chia powder. Blend until a smooth
paste has formed, stopping the machine and scraping down the sides
if needed.

In a large bowl, mix together the oats, flour, baking soda, salt, and
hemp seeds. Stir in the date mixture and mix well. Fold in the
chocolate and cacao nibs.

Spread the mixture onto the prepared baking sheet with a spatula,
forming it into a rectangle about ½-inch thick. Cut the wet dough
into about a dozen rectangles (or desired shape). Bake for 12–15
minutes, or until edges begin to turn golden brown and are cooked
through. Let cool, then separate the rectangles and serve.

**Variation:** Add in ¼ cup goji berries with the cacao nibs.

# SWEETS

*Few things are more rewarding than an over-the-top, fabulous dessert . . . that's packed with antioxidants, minerals, phytochemicals, and more! Yes, desserts with benefits. These luxuries of life are made entirely from nature's finest sweets, utilizing smart substitutions for notoriously no-no ingredients. Sacha inchi becomes a glow-giving peanut substitute; super-berries sweetly bring on the antioxidants; and, of course, cacao shines in all its energizing chocolate glory. These are sweets to celebrate.*

# DYNAMITE FUDGE

## MAKES 18 1-INCH SQUARES

*If you're looking for a way not to forget to "take" your superfoods, this recipe is the answer. Soft and full of mouth-watering sweet pleasure, this intense dark chocolate treat is deceptively fudge-like, but is actually a potent explosion of antioxidants, minerals, and beneficial phytochemicals.*

2 tablespoons maqui powder

2 tablespoons maca powder

1 tablespoons mesquite powder

6 tablespoons lucuma powder

½ cup cacao powder

¼ cup coconut sugar

6 tablespoons coconut oil

¼ cup agave nectar, or maple syrup

In a food processor or a medium bowl, mix all the dry ingredients together. Add the coconut oil and agave or maple syrup, and mix again until combined. If mixing by hand, use clean hands to knead the mixture for 1 more minute.

Place a sheet of plastic wrap on a plate and pour the mixture on top. Mold the fudge into a 1-inch thick square. Refrigerate for a minimum of 30 minutes to solidify, then slice into about eighteen 1-inch cubes. For best results, keep refrigerated and wrapped until ready to enjoy.

**Variation:** Add ½ teaspoon chlorella powder when mixing in the powders.

# ACAI BERRY TRUFFLES

### MAKES 16 TRUFFLES

*A powerfully energizing treat, these antioxidant truffles are little balls of "have a nice day." I also appreciate that the acai berry's inherent richness reduces the amount of added fat that is needed for this dessert.*

- ✻ ⅓ cup acai powder
- 1½ tablespoons coconut oil
- ✻ 2 tablespoons cacao powder
- 2 tablespoons coconut sugar
- ¾ cup (packed) soft Medjool dates (about 7 or 8), pits removed
- 1 tablespoon raw or roasted smooth almond butter
- dash sea salt
- ✻ 2 tablespoons cacao nibs

Combine all ingredients except for the cacao nibs in a food processor and process until a dense dough has formed. Add the nibs and pulse a couple of times to combine, leaving in some textural crunch.

A heaping teaspoon at a time, roll into 1-inch balls. Place on a plate and refrigerate for a minimum of 1 hour before serving. Always serve chilled, or truffles will be too soft.

**Optional:** Roll truffles in a plate of acai powder to dust exterior before refrigerating.

## SUPERFOOD TRUFFLES FOR ENERGY

The golden rule to making superfood truffles: If it's a superfood powder, it can be made into a truffle! As one of the best edible vehicles for incorporating nature's top power foods, truffles are simple to make and rewarding to eat. Just blend together a general base:

SWEET & STICKY (dates or raisins) + GOOD FAT (coconut or almond butter) + FLAVORFUL POWDER (cacao or lucuma)

Next, add additional superfood powders to taste, and roll into balls. Keep this superfood stash on hand for a bite of feel-good energy any time you need it!

# SWEET SEED CANDIES

## MAKES ABOUT 2 DOZEN CANDIES

*Similar to the traditional Greek candy "pasteli" made with honey and sesame seeds, these superfood candies take advantage of the more complex flavor and healthy benefits of yacon syrup, resulting in a crunchy and chewy (at the same time!) treat. If you cannot find pre-roasted/toasted sesame seeds, use raw ones—just pop them in the oven ahead of time for 5 minutes at 350°.*

coconut oil (for the candy tray)
½ cup yacon syrup
¼ cup hemp seeds
½ cup toasted sesame seeds

Lightly oil a baking tray with a little coconut oil.

Over medium-low heat, warm the yacon syrup for a minute until it gets bubbly. Reduce the heat to low, add the seeds, and simmer for 3–4 minutes longer, stirring constantly.

Spread the mixture onto the pre-oiled tray in about a ¼-inch layer. Let cool completely (about 15–20 minutes). Use kitchen scissors to cut into squares or desired shape.

# SACHA INCHI BUCKEYES

## MAKES ABOUT 2 DOZEN

*The second I first tasted these with my friend, we instantly locked lit-up eyes—silently communicating the same urgent message of emphatic approval. Buckeye candies are traditionally made with peanuts, but I think they provide a perfect opportunity to take advantage of sacha inchi's peanut-like flavor—and deliver a daily dose of healthy omega fats, too. These buckeyes taste a lot like peanut butter cups, but are easier to make.*

½ cup sacha inchi seeds

6 tablespoons coconut sugar

⅔ cup (packed) soft Medjool dates (about 6 or 7), pits removed

4 tablespoons raw or roasted smooth almond butter

2 tablespoons lucuma powder

½ teaspoon vanilla extract

1 batch Raw Chocolate (page 184), or 4.5 ounces of dark chocolate

In a food processor, combine all the ingredients except the chocolate and process into a crumbly dough-like consistency. Stop the machine and try rolling a sample 1-inch ball with your palms to make sure the dough is moist enough. The ball should stick together on its own, but still be on the dry side like a confection. If the dough does not stick, blend in a little water—about a teaspoon at a time—until it's just moist enough to hold together. Transfer the mixture to a bowl, and hand-roll into 1-inch balls. Place the balls on a plate and chill in the freezer for 20–30 minutes.

Chop the chocolate into little pieces, and melt it into a liquid using a double boiler method.* (If you're making a fresh batch of raw chocolate, simply follow the recipe up to the liquid stage and don't freeze it.) Remove the chilled balls from the freezer. For each buckeye, insert a toothpick into a ball, then dip the ball halfway into the molten chocolate, and remove. Since the chocolate touching the ball will begin to solidify almost immediately, give it a quick second dip to achieve a thicker chocolate layer. Carefully removing the toothpick, place the buckeye onto a large plate, chocolate side up. Repeat with remaining balls. Chill in the freezer for 15 minutes to ensure the chocolate fully hardens, then serve at room temperature.

*__Double boiler method__: Heat a large pot of water to a near boil and turn off the heat. Put the chocolate shavings into a smaller, empty pot (or metal bowl) and float on top of the water bath. Allow the shavings to slowly melt into a liquid, taking care not to get any water in the pot with the chocolate.

# RAW CHOCOLATE

## MAKES ABOUT 4.4 OUNCES (BY WEIGHT)

*Making chocolate is truly an artisan practice—stretching far beyond a simple recipe. My deep respects go to the elite chocolateers! Nonetheless, I've been more than happy to put in plenty of diligent chocolate-making time over the years, resulting in this excellent home-style method that truly works. It's simple, low in sugar, stays hard at room temperature, and conserves the quintessential chocolate taste and smooth texture, all while retaining the maximum nutrition in the cacao. And to whomever made the discovery that chocolate is good for you, I believe I'm not alone in extending a most sincere "thank you."*

½ cup solid cacao butter,
  chopped into shavings

5 tablespoons cacao powder
pinch vanilla powder, (optional)*
dash sea salt
2 tablespoons agave nectar

*Do not substitute the vanilla powder with liquid vanilla extract—it will compromise the texture of the chocolate. However, raw vanilla bean may be used.

Place a ceramic dinner plate in the freezer to chill.

Melt the cacao butter using a double boiler method: Heat a large pot of water to a near boil and turn off the heat. Put the cacao shavings into a smaller, empty pot (or metal bowl) and float on top of the water bath. Allow the shavings to slowly melt into a liquid. Take care not to get any water in the pot with the cacao butter.

Once the butter is melted, remove the pot from the hot water bath and whisk in the cacao powder, vanilla powder, and salt until combined. Add the agave, and whisk briskly for about a minute—the chocolate will begin to thicken as it cools. Grab the plate from the freezer, and spoon the chocolate on top*. Set back into the freezer and chill for about 20–30 minutes, or until chocolate is completely solid. Use a mini hard spatula or dull knife to carefully pry up and snap off chunks of the chocolate. Break into pieces. Chocolate will remain hard at a "normal" room temperature, and will soften easily when exposed to heat.

*You can also pour the chocolate into candy molds to make candy bars or smaller, decorative chocolates.

**Variation:** Use maple syrup in place of the agave nectar.

# MACA CHOCOLATE

## MAKES ABOUT 4.1 OUNCES (BY WEIGHT)

*Just a tweak of the basic Raw Chocolate recipe makes an extra-incredible,
energizing treat. Sometimes I even sneak a bite for breakfast to kick-start the day.*

½ cup solid cacao butter,
chopped into shavings

✖ 3 tablespoons cacao powder

✖ 2 tablespoons maca powder

1 ½ tablespoons agave nectar

### SUPERFOOD TIP

When making chocolate, keep everything dry! The fat molecules of the chocolate will "seize," forming a curdled texture if they come in contact with moisture—a common mistake in homemade chocolate. To avoid this problem, make sure cutting surfaces, bowls, and all utensils that the ingredients come in contact with are 100 percent dry. Also important is using a large enough bowl to melt the cacao butter in, which helps prevent it from becoming flooded with steam.

Place a ceramic dinner plate in the freezer to chill.

Melt the cacao butter using a double boiler method: Heat a large pot of water to a near boil and turn off the heat. Float a smaller, empty pot on top of the water bath, and place the cacao butter shavings inside the small pot. Allow the shavings to slowly melt into a liquid, taking care not to get any water in the pot with the cacao butter.

Once the butter is melted, remove the pot from the hot water bath and whisk in the cacao and maca powders until combined. Add the agave, and whisk again briskly for about a minute. Grab the plate from the freezer, and spoon the chocolate on top*. Set back into the freezer and chill for about 20–30 minutes, or until chocolate is completely solid. Use a mini hard spatula or dull knife to carefully pry up and snap off pieces of the chocolate. Break into pieces. Chocolate will remain hard at a "cool-to-normal" room temperature, and will soften easily when exposed to heat.

*You can also pour the chocolate into candy molds to make candy bars or smaller, decorative chocolates.

# NO-BAKE BROWNIES

*This fantastic dessert lies somewhere between a brownie and a fudge square. Made just with fruits, nuts, and pure cacao, this treat is nutritionally on par with a natural energy bar or trail mix—what a deal! (Not that you actually needed an excuse to eat a brownie.) And you can make them in less than 5 minutes, start to finish.*

1 cup (packed) soft Medjool dates (about 10 or 11), pits removed

1 cup raw walnut pieces

✳ ½ cup cacao powder

pinch sea salt

✳ 1 tablespoon—½ cup cacao nibs (use quantity to taste)

Place walnuts in a food processor and grind for a few seconds to form a coarse flour. While the machine is running, add pitted dates, cacao powder, and salt, processing until a moist, crumb-like dough has formed. Depending on the natural moisture of the dates, you may need to add a touch of water—a teaspoon at a time—to get the crumbs to "stick" when pinched together.

Spread the crumbs into an 8 × 8-inch pan, sprinkle with cacao nibs, and press firmly into a solid brownie layer. Cut into bite-size squares and serve. Alternately, press and roll brownie dough into small balls to make brownie bites.

**Variation:** Add 1 teaspoon maca powder or maqui berry powder when adding the cacao powder for an additional boost. Hemp seeds, goji berries, or other superfoods can also be sprinkled on top, to taste.

# MACA-MACAROONS

*Cookies with benefits—now that's the way to live! Easy to make and deliciously full of natural ingredients, the combination of maca and brazil nuts in these macaroons tastes almost like peanut butter . . . with a lovely coconut-ty embrace, of course. The results are quite irresistible.*

1 cup raw brazil nuts

1¼ cups unsweetened shredded coconut, plus extra for rolling

1½ tablespoons maca powder

¾ cup (packed) soft Medjool dates (about 7 or 8), pits removed

1 tablespoon maple syrup

1 tablespoon vanilla extract

¼ teaspoon sea salt

Grind all the ingredients together in a food processor until a coarse dough has formed. Check the consistency: pinch the dough and make sure that it sticks together, yet still crumbles like a cookie. If the dough is too dry, add water a teaspoon at a time until the dough sticks. If the dough is too wet, add spoonfuls of extra coconut until the dough is just right.

Form the dough into balls, about a tablespoon at a time, and roll exterior in extra coconut. Flatten into cookies and serve. Kept covered, these cookies will last several weeks.

# CHOCOLATE GOJI GRANOLA

*There's nothing subtle about this granola—it's seriously 100 percent fabulous, but resides more on the dessert-end of the spectrum than a breakfast food, which is why this recipe is in the Sweets section. That said, I openly admit to rarely waiting until dessert to sneak a handful. It also serves as my go-to movietime munchie. (Note that the recipe calls for cocoa powder and not cacao powder, just this once, for a more chocolatey flavor.)*

3 cups rolled oats*

¼ cup flaxseed powder

¼ cup unsweetened coconut flakes

2 tablespoons cocoa powder

2 tablespoons melted coconut oil

6 tablespoons applesauce

2 tablespoons agave nectar

1 tablespoon vanilla extract

½ cup (packed) soft Medjool dates (about 5 or 6), pits removed

¼ teaspoon sea salt

½ cup dried goji berries

3 tablespoons cacao nibs

½ batch Maca Chocolate (page 185), or about 2.2 ounces of store-bought dark chocolate, finely chopped

*If on a gluten-free diet, use gluten-free oats, available through natural food stores or online (see Ingredient Resources Guide on page 228).

Preheat the oven to 350° F. Line a baking sheet with parchment paper.

In a large bowl, mix together the oats, flaxseed powder, coconut flakes, and cocoa powder.

Using a single-serving (small) blender, combine the coconut oil, applesauce, agave, vanilla extract, dates, and salt. Blend into a puree. Pour the puree into the bowl with the dry mixture. Use clean hands to toss the oats thoroughly with the puree, then transfer the mixture onto the prepared baking sheet, spreading the wet granola evenly across the surface. Place in the oven and bake, setting a timer for 30 minutes. After half an hour, take the granola out of the oven and use a spatula to flip and mix the granola, using the spatula's edge to break up the large clumps to ensure even baking. Return to the oven and continue baking until the granola begins to brown, about another 20–30 minutes (50–60 minutes total baking time). Remove the hot granola from the oven, and sprinkle with the goji berries, cacao nibs, and chopped Maca Chocolate (or dark chocolate). Loosely toss the mixture to distribute the melting chocolate.

Transfer the granola temporarily to the refrigerator to cool completely and allow the chocolate to re-harden. Will last for 2–3 weeks when stored in a sealed container.

# CARAMEL APPLE COBBLER

## MAKES 8 SERVINGS

*The addition of camu powder in the "crust" gives this raw food cobbler an extra boost of vitamin C.*

2 large tart green apples, peeled, cored, and diced

2 tablespoons coconut sugar

1 teaspoon cinnamon powder

½ teaspoon allspice powder

Almond Crust

Yacon Caramel Sauce

Toss the chopped apples with the coconut sugar and spices. Divide into individual ramekins or serving bowls, crumble the Almond Crust on top, drizzle generously with the Yacon Caramel Sauce, and serve.

### ALMOND CRUST

2 cups raw almonds

✳ ½ cup flaxseed powder

1 tablespoon mesquite powder

✳ ½ teaspoon camu powder

pinch sea salt

1 cup (packed) soft Medjool dates (about 10 or 11), pits removed

1 cup soft Turkish apricots (unsulfured)

Grind the almonds into small pieces in a food processor. Add the flaxseed, mesquite, camu, and sea salt, and process until incorporated. With the machine still running, add the dates and apricots, one by one, until a chunky dough has formed—allow some of the nuts and fruit to remain coarse, providing a nice texture.

### YACON CARAMEL SAUCE

3 tablespoons yacon syrup

1 tablespoon almond butter

⅛ teaspoon sea salt

½ cup (packed) soft Medjool dates (about 5 or 6), pits removed

¼ teaspoon cinnamon powder

1 tablespoon apple juice, or water

Use a small blender to puree the yacon syrup, almond butter, salt, dates, cinnamon, and apple juice together to form a smooth, thick sauce.

### SUPERFOOD TIP

Raw food desserts (like this one) are flexible! Turn this recipe into a pie by adding a teaspoon or two of water to the crust recipe to increase stickiness. Press the dough evenly along the bottom of an 8- or 9-inch pie tin. Fill with the apple mixture, and top with the caramel sauce.

# ACAI BERRY CHEESECAKE

## MAKES ONE 9-INCH CHEESECAKE

*Acai's inherent richness is ideal for a decadent cheesecake. Loaded with antioxidants, it's truly celebratory.*

1½ cups raw cashews, soaked in water for 2 hours to soften, then drained

⅓ cup fresh lemon juice

2 tablespoons agave nectar

½ cup coconut oil, melted

½ cup acai powder

1 tablespoon lucuma powder

⅔ cup banana mash (2 or 3 bananas peeled and mashed with a fork)

1 tablespoon tahini

1 cup (packed) soft Medjool dates (about 10 or 11), pits removed

pinch sea salt

3 cups fresh blueberries, divided

Cacao-Walnut Crust

To make the cheesecake, drain the soaked cashews and discard the water. In a food processor or blender, mix together the cashews with the lemon juice, agave nectar, and coconut oil. Blend until completely smooth. Add the acai, lucuma, banana mash, tahini, dates, salt, and 1½ cups of blueberries. Blend again until smooth.

In a 9-inch springform pan, distribute the Cacao-Walnut Crust evenly and press down to form a compact flat layer. Pour the cheesecake filling on top of the crust. Cover, and place in the freezer for about an hour. Remove the chilled cake from the freezer and decorate the top with the remaining blueberries, pressing down slightly to make the berries "stick." Re-cover and freeze for another 2–3 hours. When ready to serve, release the cake from the springform pan and defrost for about 3–4 minutes to soften. Store in the freezer when not in use; will keep frozen for a few months.

## CACAO-WALNUT CRUST

1 cup cacao nibs, divided

⅔ cup raw walnuts

1 cup (packed) soft Medjool dates (about 10 or 11), pits removed

3 tablespoons lucuma powder

Set aside ⅓ cup of the cacao nibs. Place the remaining nibs, walnuts, dates, and lucuma powder in a food processor and grind until crumbly dough has formed. Check the moisture level by pinching the dough to make sure it sticks—if not, blend in a little water, a teaspoon at a time, until the sticky texture is achieved. Transfer to a bowl and mix in remaining cacao nibs. Cover until needed.

# LUCUMA ICE CREAM CUPCAKES

MAKES 12 SINGLE-SERVING ICE CREAM CUPCAKES

*Lucuma's toffee-like flavor is absolutely transcendent in ice creams, and sweet mulberries give the bottom cookie-dough layer a flavor reminiscent of angel food cake. As much as I love this recipe, the ice cream itself is so delicious that sometimes I make it à la carte and just call it a day.*

⅔ cup coconut flour

1 cup (packed) soft Medjool dates (about 10 or 11), pits removed

pinch sea salt

2 tablespoons coconut oil

1 teaspoon vanilla extract

1 cup dried mulberries

Lucuma Ice Cream

In a food processor, mix the coconut flour, dates, and salt together until a coarse powder has formed. With the machine running, add the oil and vanilla extract. Stop the machine and test the dough's consistency; it should appear dry and crumbly, but stick together easily when pressed. If it's too dry, add water, a teaspoon at a time. Once the desired consistency is achieved, add the mulberries, using the pulse button on the food processor to transform the whole berries into small bits, leaving a few larger pieces in for texture.

To assemble, line a 12-tray muffin tin with muffin cups. Add 2 heaping tablespoons of the mulberry mixture inside each cup, using the back of a spoon to press down into a firm solid layer. Dispense the Lucuma Ice Cream evenly among the cups on top of the base, cover with plastic wrap, and place in the freezer. Chill the cookie cups until ice cream is frozen through, about 2–3 hours. When ready to serve, defrost 2–3 minutes to soften.

## LUCUMA ICE CREAM

2 cups light coconut milk

1 cup (packed) soft Medjool dates (about 10 or 11), pits removed

2 frozen bananas, sliced (page 69)

½ cup lucuma powder

2 tablespoons coconut sugar

Blend all ingredients until smooth. Keep at room temperature while prepping the recipe above, or if enjoying à la carte, place in the freezer until frozen through. (An ice cream maker can also be used if available.) Defrost for 2–3 minutes before serving. Makes 1 pint.

# BANANA ICE CREAM SUNDAE

## MAKES 4 SERVINGS

*If you've never used the trick of blending frozen bananas into a gelato-like dessert, you're in for a real treat (and if you have, you know what I'm talking about!). Here, adorned with superfoods, this special version goes all out with a rich chocolate sauce, cacao nibs, and sacha inchi. This is also a perfect opportunity to get creative by adding other superfoods, or even one of the two superfood jams in this book (see pages 70 and 71) into the mix.*

10 frozen bananas (page 69)

1 tablespoon vanilla extract

Cacao Fudge Sauce

⅛ ¼ cup sacha inchi seeds, coarsely chopped

⅛ ¼ cup cacao nibs

Break the frozen bananas into chunks, and place into a food processor along with the vanilla extract. Briefly mix until a chunky-looking ice cream has formed—do not overprocess or the bananas will melt and ruin the "ice cream" effect. Refreeze until ready to use.

To serve, scoop the banana ice cream into a serving bowl, drizzle generously with the Cacao Fudge Sauce, and top with sacha inchi seeds and cacao nibs.

### CACAO FUDGE SAUCE

⅛ ⅓ cup cacao powder

1½ teaspoons mesquite powder

⅓ cup maple syrup

2 tablespoons coconut oil, melted

pinch sea salt

Mix the cacao powder, mesquite powder, maple syrup, coconut oil, and sea salt together into a smooth mixture (a single-serving blender will yield the best results). Use the sauce at room temperature* so it is easy to pour. Makes about ⅔ cup.

* This sauce may also be chilled, then used as a fantastic fudgy frosting once it cools and thickens.

---

**SUPERFOOD TIP**

Coconut oil will begin to harden below 76° F, which thickens the fudge sauce once it hits the ice cream for a fun textural effect.

---

# MAQUI-CHERRY GELATO

## MAKES 1 PINT

*If the beautiful, brilliant purple color of this gelato (thanks to the maqui) doesn't blow you away, the melt-in-your-mouth creaminess and delectable frozen yogurt-like flavor certainly will. All-natural (with no sugar added) cherry juice concentrate can be found in health food stores (if you have trouble finding it, just use regular fresh cherry juice . . . doubling the amount of juice, and adding in a few extra dates). And though maqui is the king of the antioxidant fruit world, cherries contribute many antioxidant compounds as well, resulting in a dessert with tremendous benefits. If you're a stevia fan, try using it in place of the agave nectar (to taste).*

¾ cup light coconut milk

½ cup raw cashews, soaked 2 hours in water, then drained

4 large Medjool dates, pits removed

1 tablespoon agave nectar

¼ cup cherry juice concentrate

2 tablespoons maqui powder

½ tablespoon vanilla extract

1 tablespoon lucuma powder

2 cups frozen black cherries, pitted

Use a blender to combine all the ingredients except the frozen cherries into a smooth cream. Add the cherries, and blend for just a second, until fruit is coarsely chopped but not blended smooth.

Transfer mixture to a bowl or container, cover tightly, and freeze for 4 hours or longer. Let thaw for 2–3 minutes at room temperature to soften before serving.

**Variation:** Use 3 tablespoons of acai powder in place of the maqui powder.

# VIBRANT LEMON-LIME GRANITA

## MAKES 4–6 SERVINGS

*A granita is an Italian ice—a fancier, lighter, cone-less version of a snow cone. This recipe is rewarding in two ways: its awesomely refreshing citrus flavor; and the addition of powerful wheatgrass—which is undetectable (save for its attractive green glow). Lemons and limes are also recognized as excellent detoxifiers and, combined with the wheatgrass, this dessert is almost a mini-cleanse.*

3 tablespoons fresh lime juice

2 tablespoons fresh lemon juice

⅓ cup agave nectar, or stevia to taste

2 cups water

2 teaspoons freeze-dried wheatgrass powder

### SUPERFOOD TIP

If you choose to use stevia instead of agave, aim for a sweetness that is slightly amplified to your normal taste. Cold foods diminish our taste buds' ability to perceive sweetness, so once the dessert is frozen, the sweetness will quiet down a bit.

Mix all the ingredients together in a shaker cup, glass, or blender. Pour into a large bowl or container. Cover, and place in the freezer.

After about 2 hours, remove the bowl from the freezer and use the prongs of a fork to scrape the icy mixture, separating the larger ice crystals to form a slush. Place back in the freezer and repeat twice more over the course of 3 hours to form a snow-like texture. Serve when fully frozen and "fluffy."

# STRAWBERRY ICE POPS

## MAKES 1 TRAY OF POPS (ABOUT 4–6 SERVINGS)

*A little chia goes a long way to make these ice pops a well-rounded snack, and the tiny speckled seeds make them look delightfully like giant strawberries. Using stevia cuts down on sugars and creates a healthier, low calorie sweet treat.*

2 teaspoons chia seeds
½ cup water
3 cups strawberries (fresh or frozen)
2 tablespoons fresh lemon juice
2 tablespoons agave nectar, or stevia to taste

Mix the chia seeds and water together in a glass. Let rest for 20 minutes to let the seeds plump up, stirring once about halfway through.

Place all ingredients in a blender—including the chia mixture—and blend until well combined. Pour into popsicle molds and freeze a minimum of 4 hours, or until solid.

# CACAO FUDGE POPS

## MAKES 1 TRAY OF POPS (ABOUT 4–6 SERVINGS)

*The classic, always enjoyable, frozen chocolate popsicle gets a beautiful makeover using natural ingredients. This recipe serves as a prime example of the excellent flavor partnership between mesquite and cacao—which together produce a low sugar (yet remarkably indulgent) dessert.*

¼ cup mesquite powder
¼ cup cacao powder
½ cup light coconut milk
½ cup water
2 tablespoons maple syrup

Use a blender to incorporate all ingredients. Pour into popsicle molds and freeze for a minimum of 3 hours, or until solid.

## SUPERFRUIT JUICE POPS

The days of the flourescent-colored, crazily-packaged ice pop are over. We understand there's no need to slurp down unnecessary chemical flavorings, artificial colorings, and dubious amounts of corn syrup and sugar just to quell a warm-weather dessert craving. The secret is out that great fruit ice pops can be made at home (for pennies on the dollar) with little more than a popsicle mold and natural fruit juice.

But why stop at just apple juice or lemonade? Increasingly available superfruit juices can amp up frozen treats with their exciting flavors and huge benefits. Try using acai berry juice, pure pomegranate juice, or a superfruit juice blend like Cranberry Goji (Genesis Today makes some great blends; find them in the Ingredient Resources Guide on page 228). The quick trick of mixing in a touch of stevia before freezing even further transforms these superfruits into a delicious, easy (and extra kid-friendly!) natural dessert.

# DRINKS

*Here's a whole new reason to say "cheers": easy, irresistible, and totally nutrient-packed drinks! From thick and frosty fresh smoothies to comforting homemade hot chocolate made with real cacao (and a hit of maca!), these beautiful beverages are brimming with all the best foods.*

# PIÑA COLADA SMOOTHIE

## MAKES 1 SERVING

*In this classically fabulous flavor combination, highly nutritious wheatgrass goes completely undetected, but the tremendous quantity of the enzyme bromelain in the pineapple actually increases the absorption of its beneficial nutrients. (Among its many blessings, wheatgrass is an anti-inflammatory agent and promotes wound healing!) You can use freshly cut pineapple, too—simply replace ½ cup of water with ice. Grass skirt and coconut bra is optional.*

1¼ cups frozen pineapple chunks

¼ cup light coconut milk

1 cup water

1 teaspoon freeze-dried wheatgrass powder

stevia or coconut sugar, to taste (optional)

Combine all ingredients in a blender, and process until completely smooth. Taste and adjust the sweetness, if desired, with a touch of stevia or coconut sugar.

---

### SUPERFOOD TIP

When "building" a smoothie in a blender (prior to blending), start by putting in the densest, hardest ingredients first. Following this helpful ingredient hierarchy ensures the smoothest and most efficient blending:

First: ICE (if using)
Second: FROZEN FRUITS AND/OR NUTS
Third: DRIED FRUITS AND/OR DATES
Fourth: FRESH FRUITS
Fifth: POWDERS
Last: WATER/LIQUIDS

---

# PURE & SIMPLE GREEN SMOOTHIE

## MAKES 1 BIG SERVING

*Blending vegetables mimics the beginning stages of digestion, making the nutrients in this green smoothie very accessible. Believe it or not, this smoothie tastes like tropical fruit and leaves the flavors of the mineral-rich spinach and chlorella in the backseat. Pour it into a mason jar or a big glass and proudly begin your day the green, clean way. (This smoothie has over five servings of fruits and vegetables!)*

1 cup frozen mango chunks

1 banana, peel removed

1 apple, cored and chopped

1 tablespoon lucuma powder

2 cups (packed) spinach leaves

⅛ teaspoon chlorella powder

2 cups water

stevia, to taste (optional)

Place the mango, banana, apple, lucuma powder, spinach, and chlorella into a blender. Pour in the water and blend until smooth. Taste and sweeten with stevia, if desired.

**Variation:** Super nutrient-packed chlorella has a strong flavor, though this smoothie does a good job of masking it. As you become accustomed to chlorella, feel free to add additional amounts of this superfood to your personal taste. Or use another greens powder instead, to taste (freeze-dried wheatgrass powder is excellent, too).

# SUPERBERRY SMOOTHIE

## MAKES 1–2 SERVINGS

*It's easy to enjoy the feel-good results of this fruity blend. Plus, the naturally-occurring healthy fats in the acai make it extra creamy.*

1 ½ cups frozen blueberries
1 banana, peeled
2 Medjool dates, pits removed
2 tablespoons acai powder
2 tablespoons dried goji berries
1 ½ cups cold water
ice (optional)
stevia or sweetener of choice,
   to taste (optional)

Blend all ingredients until smooth—add ice for a frostier texture. Taste and adjust sweetness, if needed.

# ORANGE MEGA-C SMOOTHIE

## MAKES 1 SERVING

*With a taste like a creamsicle, this smoothie contains almost 400 percent RDA vitamin C— a major benefit in helping to strengthen the immune system and fight free radicals.*

1 ¼ cups fresh orange juice
1 frozen banana (page 69)
2 tablespoons hemp seeds
¼ teaspoon camu powder
1 tablespoon lucuma powder
stevia or yacon syrup, to taste
ice

Blend all the ingredients together until smooth with a handful or two of ice. Taste, and adjust sweetness with stevia or yacon syrup, if needed.

# ANTIOXIDANT PARADISE SMOOTHIE

## MAKES 1–2 SERVINGS

*Boost your body's defense against aging, toxins, and degenerative disease with this delicious superfruit-packed blend. Frozen strawberries (which are especially high in vitamin C) give this smoothie a fabulous frosty feel.*

- 2 cups frozen strawberries
- 1¼ cups frozen or fresh mango, pitted, peeled, and chopped
- 1½ cups pomegranate juice
- 2 tablespoons maqui powder
- ½ cup water
- stevia or sweetener of choice, to taste (optional)

Blend all the ingredients together until smooth, adding more water if needed. Taste for sweetness and add stevia or sweetener of choice, if desired.

### SUPERFOOD TIP

Smoothies are some of the most forgiving recipes around when it comes to ingredient substitution. If you don't have an ingredient on hand, no problem: just substitute it with something similar. If the blended result doesn't meet your "fabulous" taste standards, just add a little extra of your favorite ingredients, blending again until it meets the mark. When smoothies at my house occasionally go awry (it happens), my fail-safe fixer ingredient is frozen blueberries . . . lots and lots of frozen blueberries. If the new "fixed" smoothie becomes too big to handle, I pour the remainder into ice cube trays and blend it back up the next day so as not to waste a delicious drop.

# CHOCOLATE-BERRY PROTEIN SHAKE

### MAKES 1–2 SERVINGS

*A healthy protein boost in a chocolatey-berry form. What's not to love? Although hemp protein powder (sometimes called "hemp flour") can sometimes be a little bit gritty, the trick to getting it smooth is to add plenty of ice, yielding a nice frosty texture. I love this shake after a workout to recharge (and reward!), but it also makes an ideal breakfast as an energizing way to start an extra-great day. This recipe contains around 14 grams of protein, but feel free to add more hemp protein for an even more potent shake—each tablespoon of hemp protein powder adds around 5 grams of (complete) plant-based premium protein.*

2 tablespoons raw cashews

1½ tablespoons hemp seeds

¾ cup frozen blueberries

½ frozen banana

2 Medjool dates, pits removed

2 tablespoons cacao powder

1 tablespoon hemp protein powder

1 teaspoon maca powder

1¼ cups cold water

ice

stevia or desired sweetener, to taste

Blend all the ingredients with a handful or two of ice until smooth, adding a bit more water if necessary. Taste for sweetness, adding additional sweetener if needed.

# WATERMELON CHIA FRESCA

## MAKES 1–2 SERVINGS

*A classic Mexican beverage, chia frescas are traditionally made from soaked chia seeds and water or citrus juice, with added sweetener. However, it's easy to experiment with different fresca flavors for variety, such as this juicy watermelon version. This drink is summertime's new best friend.*

1 cup water

2 teaspoons chia seeds

2½ cups chopped watermelon flesh

1½ tablespoons fresh lime juice

stevia or agave nectar, to taste (optional)

Combine the water and chia seeds in a glass and stir to combine. Let sit for 10 minutes in the refrigerator to allow the chia seeds to plump up. Stir once more, then return to the refrigerator for 10 more minutes. Place the chia mixture and all remaining ingredients in a blender and puree until well combined. Adjust the sweetness as needed. Best served chilled.

# COCONUT-LIME CHIA FRESCA

## MAKES 1–2 SERVINGS

*Hydrating coconut water extracted from "young" Thai coconuts is often used by endurance athletes because of its naturally-occurring electrolyte (mineral) content. Here, mixed with a zing of fresh lime juice and plump chia seeds, it's the ultimate thirst quencher, as well as surprisingly energizing.*

2 cups young coconut water (bottled or fresh)

2 teaspoons chia seeds

1½ tablespoons fresh lime juice

Put all the ingredients in a glass and stir to combine. Place in the refrigerator and let sit for 10 minutes to allow the chia seeds to plump up. Stir once more, then return to the refrigerator for 10 minutes longer. Best served chilled.

## SUPERFOOD TEAS

Coffee's lure of instant energy is a difficult offer to refuse. Luckily, one way to help cut the java dependency is through the use of energy-providing superfood teas. To make, simply steep a handful of superfoods (see suggestions below) in hot water for several minutes for a warm, flavorful tea. Or, make a "sun tea" infusion by allowing the superfoods to steep for an hour or two in room temperature water inside of a mason jar or glass water bottle. A bonus: after the tea is enjoyed, the plumped-up superfoods at the bottom provide a delicious snack. Here's two to try:

GOJI TEA (dried goji berries + water): sweet and pleasant, with a hint of berry
YACON TEA (dried yacon slices + water): apple-like; similar to a sweet yerba mate tea

Fresh ginger slices, lemon juice, lemon balm, lavender petals, mint leaves, and/or stevia are just a few of the many natural flavor variations that can be added to the teas above.

# HOT CHOCOLATE

MAKES 1–2 SERVINGS (2 CUPS)

*Ancient Mayan cultures were in love with making cacao drinks for energy and health. This rich and frothy hot chocolate recipe pays homage to the cultures that discovered the wonders of cacao.*

- 1 tablespoon cacao powder
- 1 teaspoon mesquite powder
- ½ teaspoon maca powder
- 2 tablespoons coconut sugar
- 2 cups cashew milk (page 224), or store-bought unsweetened almond milk

Combine all the ingredients together in a blender and blend for a minute to break down the sugar and incorporate the powders into the milk. Pour into a small saucepan and heat all the ingredients over a low stove setting until mixture is warm. Do not boil. Whisk briefly and serve in a mug.

# HOT MACA

MAKES 1 SERVING

*Creamy hot maca is an earthy, nutty, warming, and surprisingly delicious beverage—and a great way to restore energy. You can really feel the power in this one.*

- 1 teaspoon maca powder
- 1 tablespoon coconut sugar or maple syrup
- 1¼ cups cashew milk (page 224), or store-bought unsweetened almond milk

Combine all the ingredients together in a blender and blend for a minute to break down the sugar and incorporate the dry ingredients into the milk. Pour into a small saucepan and heat all the ingredients over a low stove setting until mixture is warm. Do not boil. Whisk briefly and serve in a mug.

# SPICED CAMU CIDER

## MAKES 3–4 SERVINGS (5 CUPS)

*Warm up any chilly day with a mug filled with this festive drink—enhanced by cozy spices and the antioxidant power of camu powder. Make sure to add the camu at the end of the heating process to preserve the full potential of its valuable nutrients.*

4 cups apple juice

1 cup orange juice

1 teaspoon cinnamon powder

½ teaspoon ginger powder

¼ teaspoon allspice powder

1 teaspoon camu powder

stevia or yacon syrup, to taste (optional)

Mix all ingredients except the camu together in a pot, and gently warm over low heat for 2–3 minutes until heated evenly throughout (do not boil). Remove from heat, add the camu, and mix well until camu is dissolved. Taste, and add stevia or yacon syrup for additional sweetness, if desired. Serve immediately.

## ANCESTRAL DRINKS

Drinking warm concoctions that contain nature's most healing and energizing foods is one of human-kind's oldest practices . . . perhaps our very first recipes. Not surprisingly, warm superfood drinks have a way of making us feel instinctively "good."

# CAMU BERRY LEMONADE

## MAKES ABOUT 1 QUART

*This fresh lemonade may look and taste like the classic beverage, but in fact it's loaded with vitamin C and is also low in sugar. Using a touch of agave nectar helps mask the bitterness of the camu, while most of the sweetness is carried by sugar-free and calorie-free stevia. If using stevia isn't your cup of . . . lemonade . . . then additional agave nectar (or even white grape juice) can be used; just be mindful of the overall sugars.*

⅓ cup fresh lemon juice

4 cups water

1½ tablespoons agave nectar

✳ ½ teaspoon camu powder

stevia, to taste

Mix all ingredients together, being sure the camu gets fully incorporated so there are no clumps. Sweeten with stevia to desired taste. Best served over ice.

**Variation:** For a refreshing sparkling lemonade, stir in kombucha with the lemonade mix in a 1:1 ratio.

# MAQUI BERRY LEMONADE

## MAKES ABOUT 1 QUART

*I remember loving pink lemonade as a kid, but had I seen (and tasted) this beautiful reddish-purple lemonade . . . whoa. The pink stuff wouldn't have stood a chance. This unique lemonade is rich in antioxidants with just a small hint of berry flavor from the maqui.*

⅓ cup fresh lemon juice

4 cups water

1½ tablespoons agave nectar

✳ 1 teaspoon maqui powder

stevia, to taste

Mix all ingredients together, being sure the camu gets fully incorporated so there are no clumps. Sweeten with stevia to desired taste. Best served over ice.

**Variation:** Add ½ teaspoon camu powder for the best of both lemonade worlds.

# SUPERFRUIT SANGRIA

MAKES 4–6 SERVINGS

*Sangria is a popular Spanish punch normally made from wine sweetened by an assortment of fresh fruit. Using a wide array of superfruits turns this cocktail into a potent antioxidant rainbow, with an especially high concentration of the important polyphenol resveratrol (a revered antioxidant for supporting heart health and anti-aging), which is in both the mulberries and the red wine itself. Cheers to that!*

- 2 cups frozen mixed berries
- ¼ cup dried mulberries
- ¼ cup dried goldenberries, finely chopped
- 2 tablespoons dried goji berries
- 1¼ cups pomegranate juice
- 1 bottle red wine
- 2 cups kombucha (unflavored or ginger flavor), or mineral water

Pour the fruits into a large pitcher, followed by the pomegranate juice and the wine. Refrigerate for a minimum of 5 hours or overnight to let the flavors marry—the longer the sangria sits, the better!

Just before serving, add the kombucha. Serve with or without ice, including some fruit in each glass.

**Variation:** If a sweeter wine is desired, add a touch of stevia. For a more alcoholic version, add ¼ cup brandy.

### SUPERFOOD TIP

Using frozen and dried berries instead of fresh in this type of marinated cocktail allows the natural juices and sweet flavors of the fruit to infiltrate the beverage more effectively. Plus, the wine-infused fruit has an enhanced tenderness providing a very pleasurable treat at the bottom of every glass.

PART FOUR
# EXTRAS

# SUPERFOOD SUBSTITUTION CHEAT SHEET

It happens to the best of us: ingredients run out, an item is unavailable, or maybe going to the store just seems like a little too much effort. Fortunately, many (though not all) natural ingredients can be easily substituted. Results may vary per recipe (common sense is the best ingredient of all!), but in many cases these quick subs will do the trick. Note that some substitutions are non-superfood ingredients. It's okay, though, because they're still healthy alternatives!

| SUPERFOOD | | SUBSTITUTION |
|---|---|---|
| Acai Powder | = | Maqui Powder |
| Cacao Powder | = | Cocoa Powder |
| Camu Powder | = | Omit From Recipe |
| Chlorella/Spirulina | = | Wheatgrass Powder* |
| Coconut Oil (For Cooking) | = | Safflower Oil |
| Coconut Oil (For Sweets) | = | Margarine (Trans-Fat Free) |
| Dates | = | Raisins |
| Flax Seeds/Powder | = | Chia Seeds/Powder |
| Goldenberries (Dried) | = | Dried Cranberries |
| Hemp Seeds | = | Sunflower Seeds |
| Kale | = | Swiss Chard |
| Kelp Powder | = | Dulse Flakes |
| Mesquite Powder | = | Carob Powder |
| Mulberries (Dried) | = | Raisins |
| Palm Sugar | = | Date Sugar or Sucanat |
| Pomegranate Juice | = | Cranberry Juice |
| Quinoa | = | Millet or Brown Rice |
| Raspberries | = | Blackberries |
| Sacha Inchi Seeds | = | Macadamia Nuts |
| Strawberries | = | Blueberries |
| Ume Plum Vinegar | = | Shoyu + Lemon Juice |
| Wakame | = | Sea Palm or Omit |
| Watercress | = | Arugula |
| Yacon (Dried Slices) | = | Dried Apple Slices |
| Yacon Syrup | = | Date Syrup or Agave (Use ½) |

*A good multi-greens powder may also be used.

# CONVERSION CHART

**NON-LIQUID INGREDIENTS** (Weights of common ingredients in grams)

| INGREDIENT | 1 CUP | ¾ CUP | ⅔ CUP | ½ CUP | ⅓ CUP | ¼ CUP | 2 TBSP |
|---|---|---|---|---|---|---|---|
| Butter Spread | 240 g | 180 g | 160 g | 120 g | 80 g | 60 g | 30 g |
| Chia | 163 g | 122 g | 108 g | 81 g | 54 g | 41 g | 20 g |
| Chopped fruits and vegetables | 150 g | 110 g | 100 g | 75 g | 50 g | 40 g | 20 g |
| Coconut oil | 216 g | 162 g | 144 g | 108g | 72 g | 54 g | 27 g |
| Couscous, uncooked | 180 g | 135 g | 120 g | 90 g | 60 g | 45 g | 22 g |
| Dates, chopped | 151 g | 117 g | 100 g | 75 g | 50 g | 39 g | 19 g |
| Goji berries | 111 g | 83 g | 74 g | 55 g | 37 g | 28 g | 14 g |
| Nuts, chopped | 150 g | 110 g | 100 g | 75 g | 50 g | 40 g | 20 g |
| Nuts, ground | 120 g | 90 g | 80 g | 60 g | 40 g | 30 g | 15 g |
| Parmesan cheese, grated | 90 g | 65 g | 60 g | 45 g | 30 g | 22 g | 11 g |
| Sea salt, crystals | 269 g | 202 g | 179 g | 135 g | 90 g | 67 g | 34 g |

Note: Non-liquid ingredients specified in American recipes by volume (if more than about 2 tablespoons or 1 fluid ounce) can be converted to weight with the table above. If you need to convert an ingredient that isn't in this table, the safest thing to do is to measure it with a traditional measuring cup and then weigh the results with a metric scale. In a pinch, you can use the volume conversion table below.

**VOLUME CONVERSIONS** (Used for liquids)

| CUSTOMARY QUANTITY | METRIC EQUIVALENT |
|---|---|
| 1 teaspoon | 5 mL |
| 1 tablespoon or ½ fluid ounce | 15 mL |
| 1 fluid ounce or ⅛ cup | 30 mL |
| ¼ cup or 2 fluid ounces | 60 mL |
| ⅓ cup | 80 mL |
| ½ cup or 4 fluid ounces | 120 mL |
| ⅔ cup | 160 mL |
| 1 cup or 8 fluid ounces or ½ pint | 250 mL |
| 1½ cups or 12 fluid ounces | 350 mL |
| 2 cups or 1 pint or 16 fluid ounces | 475 mL |
| 3 cups or 1½ pints | 700 mL |
| 4 cups or 2 pints or 1 quart | 950 mL |
| 4 quarts or 1 gallon | 3.8 L |

Note: In cases where higher precision is not justified, these conversions can be rounded off as follows:

| | |
|---|---|
| 1 cup = 250 mL | |
| 1 pint = 500 mL | |
| 1 quart = 1 L | |
| 1 gallon = 4 L | |

**WEIGHT CONVERSIONS**

| CUSTOMARY QUANTITY | METRIC EQUIVALENT |
|---|---|
| 1 ounce | 28 g |
| 4 ounces or ¼ pound | 113 g |
| ⅓ pound | 150 g |
| 8 ounces or ½ pound | 230 g |
| ⅔ pound | 300 g |
| 12 ounces or ¾ pound | 340 g |
| 1 pound or 16 ounces | 450 g |
| 2 pounds | 900 g |

Note: Ounces referred to in this table are not the same as fluid ounces.

# MAKING NUT & SEED MILKS

Homemade nut and seed milks couldn't be easier . . . or healthier. Simply blended with water, many types of nuts and seeds transform into a deliciously creamy beverage that can be used just like dairy, while offering beautiful flavor subtleties. New varieties of nut milks are increasingly available in stores, but making them at home offers clear advantages: a fresher, less expensive product with cleaner ingredients (no preservatives needed). A smart addition to natural recipes, homemade nut milks last about a week, refrigerated.

| NUT/SEED* | QUANTITY | WATER** | SOAK TIME |
|---|---|---|---|
| Almonds | ¼ cup | 1¼ cups | 6+ hours |
| Cashews | ¼ cup | 1¼ cups | 2+ hours |
| Hazelnuts | ¼ cup | 1¼ cups | 6+ hours |
| Hemp seeds | ¼ cup | 1¼ cups | 1+ hours |
| Macadamia nuts | ¼ cup | 1½ cups | 4+ hours |
| Sesame seeds | ¼ cup | 1 cup | 1+ hours |
| Sunflower seeds | ⅓ cup | 1½ cups | 2+ hours |

*Use raw nuts/seeds for best flavor and health. **Water used for blending (not soak water).

## METHOD ONE (SLOWER METHOD, BEST PRODUCT)
Soak, then rinse the nuts or seeds in plenty of water (soak water quantity is not important, as long as it covers the nuts/seeds). Pre-soaking ensures easier blending and a smoother milk. Use a blender to mix the soaked ingredients and measured water (see chart) into a smooth cream. Depending on the power of your blender, this can take anywhere from 20 seconds to several minutes. Use a fine mesh sieve or cheesecloth (or nut milk bag if you have one) to strain out any large particulates.

## METHOD TWO (FASTER METHOD, THINNER PRODUCT)
Skip the soaking entirely, and blend the raw nuts or seeds with the water. If a smoother viscosity is desired, strain the liquid before using a sieve, cheesecloth, or nut milk bag.

## NUT MILK VARIATIONS
For creams: reduce the water by half. Conversely, use additional water for "skim" milk.
For sweet milks: blend in a pitted date or two, or add a little stevia.
For flavored milks: add spices like cinnamon, powders like cacao, or extracts like vanilla.

# FREQUENTLY ASKED QUESTIONS

**Is Superfood Kitchen *a diet cookbook? Can I expect to lose (or gain) weight from eating superfoods?***

I do not consider consuming superfoods and whole foods a "diet" in the conventional sense of the word. Nonetheless, there are many benefits that naturally accompany this lifestyle that many "diets" attempt. These benefits can include diminished cravings (for "junk" food), increased energy, clear skin, and, indeed, a balanced weight. Although this way of eating is not a calorie-counting method (or restrictive in any of the macronutrient departments), most natural foods have a lower caloric content and higher "bulk" than their refined food counterparts. Many people find that in addition to feeling great, a consistent inclusion of whole, plant-based foods promotes looking great, too.

**There's a lot of ingredients listed that I've never seen before. Where can I find them?**

As mentioned in the third chapter, a quick call to your local health food store can solve the question of whether the ingredients you're seeking are available nearby. Some stores will even place a special order; remember, they're here to serve you, the customer—so don't be shy about requesting that they carry a product you're looking for. Personally, however, I'm a big fan of the ease of ordering online. All superfood ingredients used in this book are listed in the Ingredient Resources Guide (page 228) for simple and direct ordering.

**Why do some superfoods cost more than other kinds of "regular" foods?**

Producing a superfood crop that is grown organically and processed with care, and paying farmers and workers fairly for their efforts all contribute to driving up the price.

It's also important to recognize that within the mind-set of "calories-per-dollar," the conventional diet might seem like a better bargain, but the *nutrient*-per-dollar ratio is frighteningly low. Considering the high concentration of benefits that reside in superfoods, it's clear that superfoods may not be as expensive as they seem. A small package of freeze-dried wheatgrass, for example, may cost around seven times more than a box of cereal. Yet each tiny half-teaspoon of wheatgrass contains over 70 nutrients (the nutrition of a humongous green salad, or more), and there's likely a one or two months' supply in each bag.

Ominous and sensationalized statements aside, we genuinely do have the choice to pay now or pay later when it comes to our health.

### How should superfood ingredients be stored?

It depends upon the ingredient. I'm a big fan of keeping lots of inexpensive (and reusable) glass mason jars around to keep "long-term" foods in, especially if the food comes in plastic packaging. Superfood powders, seeds, dried berries, and other "bulk" items can be stored this way at room temperature, away from direct sunlight. If you think you may not go through nuts or seeds very quickly, keep them in the refrigerator. Also, when refrigerating sprouts, make sure a little air can get into the bag or container—the sprouts will last much longer this way.

### Why are there no animal products (meat/dairy/eggs) used in any of the recipes?

Because the nutritional benefits of each and every ingredient are a fundamental principle to the formulation of these recipes, there are many ingredients that instantly go on the "excluded" list. This list includes white flour, refined white sugar and high fructose corn syrup, all highly processed ingredients, and indeed, all animal products. Because animal products (meat, fish, dairy/dairy products, and eggs) have been well-documented to have numerous unhealthy components that contribute to the leading diseases of our time (including heart disease, diabetes, osteoporosis, and cancer), this food group as a whole directly contradicts the philosophy of superfood cuisine. Even organic and "free-range" meats and animal products—while better than their factory-farmed counterparts—still invite disease and health problems.

A weighted issue, there are a plethora of excellent books, films, and studies on the subject of animal-derived food and its impact on long-term health (see Further Reading, page 230). Once faced with the undeniable truths of modern science, it's easy to understand why incorporating as many plant-based whole food recipes as possible is among the very best ways to be good to your body.

### Many superfoods are grown in other parts of the world. What about eating locally grown food?

The local food movement is one that I thoroughly believe in and stand behind. Depending on where you live, it is extremely satisfying to engage in buying fresh produce that's been grown nearby— boosting the local economy and reducing the resources needed for the transportation of goods. Unfortunately for North Americans like myself, superfoods are largely not a local specialty. Does this mean we should not consume them?

I don't believe it's a black-and-white issue. Though many superfoods are indigenous to other countries, North America's diverse climate has the potential to grow many of these foods on home soil. Currently, the reason why more superfoods are not grown locally is connected to demand. While North America has thousands of uses for certain crops, like corn, the perceived market for "newer foods," like goji berries, is still relatively small. When, as consumers, we can prove to our farmers (and our government) that a strong demand exists for these nutrient-dense super-crops, we may see a shift in the foods that are grown locally. In the meantime, the fair exchange of goods and services from our global neighbors remains a beneficial practice, and in the case of superfoods, one that often strengthens struggling farming communities, providing stable income for women and families.

# INGREDIENT RESOURCES GUIDE

## NAVITAS NATURALS

Specializing in 100 percent organic superfoods that are minimally processed, gluten-free, kosher, and certified for food safety, Navitas Naturals is an industry-leading source for about 80 percent of the non-perishable superfoods used in this book. They maintain direct relationships with their farmers and packers, support fair trade practices, and are a green company. A top-quality resource.

Visit: **navitasnaturals.com**

**Find here:** Acai powder, camu powder, cacao products (powder, nibs, cacao butter, and more), chia seed, sprouted chia seed powder, sprouted flaxseed powder, goji berries, goldenberries, hemp seed, hemp protein powder, lucuma powder, maca powder, maqui powder, mulberries, nori sheets, coconut sugar, freeze-dried wheatgrass powder, dried yacon slices, yacon syrup, and more.

## SEQUEL NATURALS

Sequel Naturals is an excellent functional food company featuring plant-based superfood products as well as an award-winning, health-optimizing line called Vega. This line includes Vega Antioxidant EFA Oil, which is the best culinary oil—in taste and nutrition—I've ever come across.

Visit: **sequelnaturals.com**

**Find here:** Vega Antioxidant EFA Oil (a plant-based mixture of hemp oil, flax oil, and several raw antioxidant oils), sacha inchi (sold as SaviSeed—use the "Oh Natural" variety for the recipes in this book), chlorella powder (sold as ChlorEssence), and more.

## MAINE COAST SEA VEGETABLES

This company offers sustainably harvested wild sea vegetables from the North Atlantic. Due to their experienced propagation of native species, protection of clean coastal waters, and regular testing to ensure product quality and purity, this company's array of raw, certified-organic, dried sea ingredients is of truly premium quality. In addition to selling in stores, they also offer certain items in bulk online.

Visit: **seaveg.com**

**Find here:** Dulse (strips and flakes), kelp granules (powder), wakame flakes (sold as alaria), and more.

## QUINOA CORPORATION

The go-to source for all things quinoa. Featuring certified organic ingredients, Quinoa Corporation was the first company to bring quinoa into the United States through the natural foods industry, and has since done wonders to spread the word about the amazing benefits of this seed.

Visit: **quinoa.net**

**Find here:** Quinoa (yellow, red, and black varieties), quinoa flakes, quinoa flour, quinoa pasta, and more.

## BOB'S RED MILL

With over 400 products, Bob's Red Mill Natural Foods carries just about every kind of flour (including gluten-free options) and whole grain you can imagine. They offer an extensive array of organic products too, which I strongly recommend choosing when available.
Visit: **bobsredmill.com**

**Find here:** Oat flour (gluten-free available), whole wheat flour, gluten-free flour mix, unsweetened coconut flakes, coconut flour, ground flaxseed, rolled oats (gluten-free available), nutritional yeast, and more.

## FRONTIER NATURAL PRODUCTS CO-OP

Sold under the Frontier Natural Products Co-op and Simply Organic brands, this broad line of natural and organic products includes culinary herbs, spices, and baking flavors/extracts. In addition to consistently offering excellent quality, I especially love this company for their efforts in supporting and promoting social and environmental responsibility. Many items are offered in bulk as well as the smaller sizes; buy organic when available.
Visit: **frontiercoop.com**

**Find here:** Dried herbs (huge variety), seasonings, and extracts.

## NUNATURALS

Although there are many brands of stevia on the market, NuNaturals is among the best. Their stevia products are known and loved for lacking the bitter aftertaste that can sometimes occur with lower-end stevia products. Even more helpful, NuNaturals offers many different forms of stevia for a variety of applications. I find the clear liquid stevia is the easiest way to control the quantity used.
Visit: **nunaturals.com**

**Find here:** Powdered stevia, liquid stevia, flavored stevia, and more.

## GENESIS TODAY

Genesis Today's tagline, "food with purpose," is missing a word in the beginning: delicious. This extensive line of superfruit juices, juice blends, and coconut water is not only tasty, it's also devoid of added sugars (everything is simply sweetened with juice) and brimming with top-notch power foods. Genesis Today also has a line of pure superfood supplements like pure liquid cacao (potent!) and other specialty superfoods. They serve as a convenient and easy way to both begin and maintain a superfood lifestyle; check their online store locator to find them at a retailer near you.
Visit: **genesistoday.com**

**Find here:** Sea buckthorn juice, coconut water, super-fruit juices (a large selection including acai juice, cranberry-goji juice, and pomegranate-berry juice), liquid superfood supplements, and more.

## JULIEMORRIS.NET/SHOP

In addition to these great resources, you're also welcome to visit my personal online store. Here you can directly shop my pantry—which includes superfood and natural food ingredients, kitchen tools, books, and more—all in one convenient place.

# FURTHER READING

## WEBSITES

**choosingraw.com**
Choosing Raw is a wonderful blog with healthy recipes and tips, featuring fresh content daily.

**crazysexylife.com**
An exuberant approach to health and the prevention of disease, featuring expert guest bloggers.

**eatrightamerica.com**
An inspiring organization; find more superfood information and the ANDI chart in full here.

**forksoverknives.com**
This website associated with the feature film of the same name examines the profound claim that most, if not all, degenerative diseases can be controlled by including more plant-based whole foods.

**gliving.com**
A treasure of natural recipes, videos, and eco design.

**mindbodygreen.com**
A great source for in-the-know health and eco news.

**thekindlife.com**
A lovely website that makes a natural lifestyle fun.

**TED.com**
For ideas.

## BOOKS

*Becoming Raw* by Brenda Davis, RD, and Vesanto Melina, MS, RD, with Rynn Berry. A vast and comprehensive compilation on the nutrition of raw, plant-based, whole foods.
**brendadavisrd.com**

*Nutritarian Handbook* by Joel Fuhrman, MD. A dietary overview using the ANDI system and nutrient density ratio for optimum health.
**drfuhrman.com**

*Superfoods* by David Wolfe. A fun and inspiring approach to eating nature's premium foods.
**davidwolfe.com**

*The China Study* by T. Colin Campbell, PhD, and Thomas M. Campbell II. A look at the link between nutrition and heart disease, diabetes, and cancer.
**thechinastudy.com**

*The pH Miracle* by Robert O. Young, PhD, and Shelly Redford Young. The complex subject of acid versus alkaline foods demystified.
**phmiracle.com**

*Thrive* (or *The Thrive Diet* in Canada) by Brendan Brazier. A life-changing read on how plant-based foods can enhance performance, energy, and health.
**brendanbrazier.com**

# REFERENCES

Campbell, T. Colin, PhD, and Thomas M. Campbell II. *The China Study.* Dallas, TX: BenBella Books, Inc., 2006.

"Chlorella—The Facts." Complete Spirulina and Chlorella Resource Center. www.spirulinachlorella.com/ chlorellafact.html

Collins, Karen, R.D. "Berries: Cancer-fighting super foods?" MSNBC. 9 Aug. 2006. www.msnbc.msn.com/id/13484206/

Davis, Brenda, RD, and Vesanto Melina, MS, RD, and Rynn Berry. *Becoming Raw: The Essential Guide to Raw Vegan Diets.* Summertown, TN: Book Publishing Company, 2010.

Fuhrman, Joel, MD. *Eat To Live: The Revolutionary Formula for Fast and Sustained Weight Loss.* New York, NY: Little, Brown and Company, 2003.

Gurshe, Siegfried. *Fantastic Flax.* Summertown, TN: Alive Books, 1999.

Hill, Amelia. "Forget superfoods, you can't beat an apple a day." The Observer. 13 May 2007. www.guardian.co.uk/uk/2007/may/13/health. healthandwellbeing1

Holford, Patrick. *The New Optimum Nutrition Bible.* Berkeley, CA: The Crossing Press, 2004.

Joyce, Christopher. "Ancient Figs May Be First Cultivated Crops." NPR. 2 Jun. 2006. www.npr.org/templates/story/story/ph2?storyId= 5446137

Kamozawa, Aki, and H. Alexander Talbot. *Ideas In Food: Great Recipes And Why They Work.* New York: Clarkson Potter/Publishers, 2010.

"Measuring the Nutrient Density of your Food." Eat Right America. www.eatrightamerica.com/nutritarian-lifestyle/ Measuring-the-Nutrient-Density-of-your-Food

Meyerowitz, Steve. *Sprouts: The Miracle Food.* Summertown, TN: Book Publishing Company, 1999.

"Micronutrients." World Health Organization. www.who.int/nutrition/topics/micronutrients/en/

"Mulberries the latest 'superfruit.'" Natural Actives. 1 Oct. 2008. http://naturalactives.com/mulberries-anti-ageing-superfood

Page, Linda, Ph.D. *Linda Page's 12th Edition Healthy Healing: A Guide to Self-Healing for Everyone.* Healthy Healing, Inc., 2004.

Pollan, Michael. *In Defense of Food: An Eater's Manifesto.* New York, NY: Penguin, 2008.

Stephey, M.J. "Eating Your Veggies: Not As Good For You?" Time. 18 Feb. 2009. www.time.com/time/health/article/0,8599,1880145,00 .html

Townsley, Graham. "Becoming Human Part 2." PBS. 10 Nov. 2009. www.pbs.org/wgbh/nova/evolution/becoming -human-part-2.html

Ulster University. "Watercress: Anti-Cancer Superfood." Medical News Today. 18 Feb. 2007. www.medicalnewstoday.com/articles/63314.php

Wolfe, David, and Shazzie. *Naked Chocolate.* San Diego, CA: Maul Brother's Publishing, 2005.

# ACKNOWLEDGMENTS

*Thank you:*

To my mom, Jackie Morris, for being amazing in general, but also for being an amazing book editor on the first edition. You've read this cookbook more times than anyone should have to read *any* book, ever. Your love and literary judgment helped strengthen every single aspect of this book. It has meant the world to me to work side-by-side with you on this project, a proud fact I will treasure forever.

To my dad, Rick Morris, for all your support and love, advice and wisdom, humor and pizazz. Thank you for supplying your awesome talents to help produce my cooking videos, and also tolerating decades-worth of monstrous messes in your kitchen along the way.

To Brendan Brazier, for being my solid (but compassionate) rock, and partner-in-crime. Your perspective, insight, and wit are invaluable to me; it's been wonderful to munch through this cookbook with you.

To Wes Crain and Zach Adelman at Navitas Naturals, for believing in and sponsoring this project; I feel infinitely lucky to work with such good people. A million thank you's.

To Marilyn Allen, for lighting the wick on my creative candle and leading the way to opportunity—you are a true blessing!

To the phenomenal team at Sterling, for bringing me into your publishing family . . . and for all the heaping ounces of extra awesome you poured into this book! My heartfelt thanks to my seriously wonderful-in-every-sense editor Jennifer Williams, the lovely organizational guru Sasha Tropp, Christine Heun for the savvy visual nips and tucks, and Kim Marini for keeping everything flowing! I'm so grateful to work with all of your talents; thank you for coaxing this book into its very best form.

To my Nama, Evelyn Morris, for all your seasoned cooking advice; you are a fountain of knowledge and love.

To Gena Hamshaw, for all the articulate feedback and premium supply of sass.

To Jeremiah Kent, for providing encouragement and inspiration from the start.

To all the *Superfood Kitchen* recipe testers and tasters, thank you for volunteering your time and your taste buds, and for providing your valuable and constructive critiques.

And to all the organic farmers of the world, thank you for tending to our food and our land with such care.

# INDEX